Pick and Choose

Pick and Choose

Multiple choice comprehension passages

ROBERT BEST

LONGMAN

LONGMAN GROUP LIMITED
London

Associated companies, branches and representatives throughout the world

First published 1971
*New impressions *1971 (twice);*
**1972 (twice); *1973; *1974*
**1976; *1977*

ISBN 0 582 52317 6

Printed in Hong Kong by
Dai Nippon Printing Co (H.K.) Ltd

Contents

Acknowledgements

We are grateru to the following for permission to reproducc copyright material:

The Bodley Head and Harcourt Brace Jovanovich, Inc., for an extract from *One Man's Mexico* by John Lincoln, copyright © 1967 by John Lincoln; author's agents for an extract from *Travel in England* by Thomas Burke; Jonathan Cape Limited and the Estate of Hugh Dormer for an extract from *Hugh Dormer's Diaries*; Chatto and Windus Limited for an extract from *Reputation for a Song* by Edward Grierson; Collins Publishers and Harper and Row, Publishers, Inc., for an extract from *The White South* by Hammond Innes (United States title *The Survivors,* copyright 1949 by Ralph Hammond Innes); author and author's agents for an extract from *The Arabian Knight* by Seton Dearden; Hamish Hamilton Limited and Mrs James Thurber for an extract from 'The Dog that Bit People' by James Thurber from *Vintage Thurber,* copyright © 1963 Hamish Hamilton, London, and *My Life and Hard Times,* copyright © 1933, 1961, James Thurber, published by Harper and Row, New York; author and author's agent for an extract from *The Year of the Lion* by Gerald Hanley; William Heinemann Limited and Harper and Row, Publishers, Inc., for an extract from *Ossian's Ride* by Fred Hoyle, copyright © 1959 by Fred Hoyle; Hodder and Stoughton Limited and Alfred A. Knopf, Inc., for an extract from *Cause for Alarm* by Eric Ambler; Hodder and Stoughton Limited and J. B. Lippincott Company for an extract from *The Colditz Story* by P. R. Reid, copyright 1952 by P. R. Reid; author and author's agents for an extract from *Goodbye to All That* by Robert Graves, copyright © 1957 by Robert Graves; author, author's agent, Michael Joseph Limited and Little, Brown and Company for an extract from *Rogue Male* by Geoffrey Household, copyright 1939 Geoffrey Household; Hutchinson Publishing Group Limited and author's agents for an extract from *The Pumpkin Eater* by Penelope Mortimer, © 1962 by Penelope Mortimer; Macmillan and Company Limited and St Martin's Press, Inc., for an extract from *The Price of Glory—Verdun* by Alistair Horne; author's agents, Trinity College, Oxford, Hodder and Stoughton Limited and Doubleday and Company, Inc., for an extract from *The House of the Arrow* by A. E. W. Mason; The Literary Executor of W. Somerset Maugham, William Heinemann Limited and Doubleday and Company, Inc., for an extract from *Ashenden* by W. Somerset Maugham, copyright 1927 by Somerset Maugham; author, author's agents and Doubleday & Company, Inc., for an extract from *The Parasites* by Daphne du Maurier, copyright 1949 by D. D. Browning; author, author's agents and Alfred A. Knopf, Inc., for an extract from *The Cruel Sea* by Nicholas Monserrat; Oxford University Press for an extract from *The Man-Eaters of Kumaon* by Jim Corbett; author's agents for an extract from *The Five Red Herrings* by Dorothy Sayers; The Trustees of the Estate of Nevil Shute Norway, William Heinemann Limited and William Morrow and Company Inc., for an extract from *No Highway* by Nevil Shute, copyright 1948 by William Morrow and Company, Inc.; University of Cambridge Local Examinations Syndicate for a passage from Lower Certificate English Composition and Language Paper June, 1962. We have been unable to trace the copyright holder of *Seven Years in Tibet* by Heinrich Harrer and would appreciate any information that would enable us to do so.

Introduction

This book consists of twenty-seven passages for the use of foreign students studying English at intermediate level. The general standard of the passages is that of the Cambridge First Certificate Examination, but the author has chosen and arranged them so that, within this level, they become increasingly difficult as the student progresses through the book.

Most of the vocabulary and constructions in the passages are within the range of at least the passive knowledge of students at the level in question. Where words occur which may be outside this range the author has, in order to preserve the difficulties encountered in reading in real life, purposely avoided 'doctoring' the text. Care has been taken, however, to ensure either that the passages are such that they can be understood without knowledge of the difficult words, or that the meaning of the latter can be worked out by reference to the context.

Each passage is followed by multiple choice exercises. The questions in these exercises are of two types, one designed to test comprehension, the other, knowledge of structure, vocabulary and idiom. The questions of the first type correspond to those to be found in the Reading Comprehension paper of the Cambridge First Certificate Examination, while those of the second type will be found useful in preparing for the Use of English paper in the same examination. (In the first type only one choice is correct in each question; in the questions of the second type there may be several correct choices.)

In addition, there is at the end of each set of questions a further question which requires the student to pick out certain facts or incidents in each passage and set them down in his own words in simple continuous prose.

1 *A place to live*

We gave the Masefields notice that the cottage would be free by the end of June quarter 1921; but did not have any idea where to go, or what to do next. It seemed clear that we must get another cottage somewhere, live quietly, look after the children ourselves, and try to make what money we needed by writing and drawing. Nancy, who had taken charge of everything while I was ill, now set me the task of getting the cottage. It must be found in three weeks' time.

I protested: 'But you know there isn't a single cottage for rent anywhere.'

'Yes, but we simply *have* to get one.'

'All right, then, describe it in detail. Since there are no cottages, we might as well get something that we really like.'

'Well, it must have six rooms, water indoors, a beamed attic, a walled-in garden, and it must be near the river. It must be in a village with shops, and yet a little removed from the village. The village must lie five or six miles from Oxford in the opposite direction from Boar's Hill. The church must have a tower and not a spire – I've always hated spires. And we can afford only ten shillings a week unfurnished.'

I took down other details about soil, sanitation, windows, stairs, and kitchen sinks; laid a ruler across the Oxford Ordnance map, and found five riverside villages which corresponded in general direction and distance with Nancy's stipulation. Of these five villages, two proved on inquiry to possess shops; and, of these two, one had a towered church and the other a spired church.

I went to a firm of house-agents in Oxford and asked: 'Have you any cottages to let unfurnished?'

The clerk laughed politely. 'What I want is a cottage just outside the village of Islip, with a walled garden, six rooms, water in the house, a beamed attic, and at a rent of ten shillings a week.'

'Oh, you mean the World's End cottage? But that's for sale, not for rent. However, it's failed to find a buyer for two years, so perhaps the owner will let it go now at five hundred pounds, which is only half of what he originally asked.'

The next day Nancy came to Islip with me. She looked around and said: 'Yes, this is the cottage all right, but I shall have to cut down the cypress trees, and change those window-panes. We'll move in on quarter-day.'

'But the money! We haven't the money.'

Nancy answered: 'If we could find the exact house, surely we can find a mere lump sum of money?'

She was right. My mother very kindly bought the cottage for five hundred pounds and let it to us at ten shillings a week.

from *Goodbye to All That* by ROBERT GRAVES

In questions (i) to (xii) only one choice is correct.

(i) The writer protested to Nancy about the task she had set him, because
A. he had been ill
B. there were no cottages to let anywhere
C. they had to have a cottage
D. there was no cottage he really liked

(ii) He asked Nancy to describe it in detail, because
A. he needed to draw it
B. they simply had to get one in three weeks' time
C. he wanted to know what kind of cottage would suit Nancy
D. there was no cottage really like it

(iii) He laid a ruler across the Oxford Ordnance map, in order to
A. find the general direction of Oxford
B. find any villages five or six miles from Oxford
C. measure the Ordnance map
D. measure the distance between the five villages

(iv) The clerk thought the owner would
A. allow it to be sold at five hundred pounds
B. allow it to be rented at half the original cost
C. leave it for two years
D. find a buyer in two years

(v) They simply *had* to get a cottage because
A. the writer had been ill

B. they were due to leave the one they were living in
C. they needed money
D. they had so many children

(vi) 'two villages proved on inquiry to possess shops' (l. 25) means
A. he went into shops in two of the villages to ask some questions
B. two villages had asked about shops
C. he approved of two villages for asking about shops
D. he discovered by asking people that two of the villages had shops

(vii) 'free' (l. 1) means
A. rent-free
B. without an owner
C. ready to let
D. for sale

(viii) 'in three weeks' time' (ll. 7–8) means
A. after three weeks
B. not before three weeks had passed
C. within three weeks
D. three weeks later

(ix) 'let it go' (l. 34) means
A. let it
B. leave it
C. sell it
D. rent it

(x) 'it's failed to find a buyer for two years' (l. 33) means that for two years
A. a buyer lost it
B. it has not had an owner
C. a buyer has been looking for it
D. it has been for sale

(xi) 'corresponded with Nancy's stipulation' (ll. 23–24) means
A. was what Nancy wanted
B. replied to the letter Nancy wrote to them
C. Nancy had visited
D. Nancy told me to visit

(xii) 'all right' (l. 37) means
A. without doubt
B. in good condition

C. well designed
D. perhaps

To answer the following, write down the number of the question and the letter of every item that could fill the gap. The items you choose must be grammatically correct and must correspond to the meaning in the original passage.

(xiii) ...... I was ill Nancy had taken charge of everything.

A. During the time
B. Meanwhile
C. In the time
D. By the time

(xiv) Nancy now left it to me ...... the cottage.
A. for getting
B. getting
C. to get
D. in order to get

(xv) There are no cottages, ... we might as well get something we really like.
A. so
B. therefore
C. in that case
D. as

(xvi) I asked whether ...... any cottages to let.
A. they have
B. they were having
C. they had had
D. they had

(xvii) The owner ...... to sell it for two years.
A. was unable
B. has not succeeded
C. has been unable
D. is unable

Rewrite the following sentences according to the instructions after each. Change the meaning as little as possible. Change only enough to do what you are asked to and to make a correct sentence.

(xviii) 'Nancy, who had taken charge of everything while I was ill, now set me the task of getting the cottage.'
Begin: 'While I was ill ......'

(xix) 'However, it's failed to find a buyer for two years, so perhaps the owner will let it go now at five hundred pounds.'

Begin: 'Perhaps the owner ......'

(xx) Describe, in about 80 words, what Nancy did, without quoting her actual words at any point.

2 *Adventures of a secret agent*

Ashenden, the British Agent in Geneva in World War I, was bitterly disappointed. His attempt to get Chandra Lal, the German Agent, to come to Thonon, in answer to a letter from the woman he loved, had failed. Instead of coming, Chandra sent her a letter which Ashenden had intercepted.

Then Ashenden had an inspiration. He said to Felix, his French colleague: 'Find the man who brought this letter. Tell him to return to the person who gave it to him. He is to say that he took it to the lady and she sent it back. If the person asks him to take another letter he is to say that it is not much good as she is packing her trunk and leaving Thonon.'

He saw the letter handed over and the instructions given and then walked back to his little house in the country.

The next boat on which Chandra could possibly come arrived about five and having at that hour an important engagement with an agent working in Germany, he warned Felix that he might be a few minutes late. But if Chandra came he could easily be detained; there was no great hurry since the train in which he was to be taken to Paris did not start till shortly after eight. When Ashenden had finished his business he strolled leisurely down to the lake. It was light still and from the top of the hill he saw the steamer pulling out. It was an anxious moment and instinctively he quickened his steps. Suddenly he saw someone running towards him and recognized the man who had taken the letter.

'Quick, quick,' he cried. 'He's there.'

Ashenden's heart gave a great thud against his chest.

'At last.'

He began to run too and as they ran the man, panting, told him how he had taken back the unopened letter. When he put it in Chandra's hand the latter turned frightfully pale, and turned it over and over in his hand as though he could not understand what his own letter was doing there. Tears sprang to his eyes and rolled down his cheeks. He said something in a language the man did not understand and then in French asked him when the boat went to Thonon. When the man got on board he looked about, but did not see Chandra; then he caught sight of him, huddled up in a coat with his hat drawn down over his eyes, standing alone in the bows. During the crossing he kept his eyes fixed on Thonon.

'Where is he now?' asked Ashenden.

'I got off first and Monsieur Felix told me to come for you.'

'I suppose they're holding him in the waiting-room.'

Ashenden was out of breath when they reached the pier. He burst into the waiting-room. A group of men, talking at the top of their voices and gesticulating wildly, were clustered round a man lying on the ground.

'What's happened?' he cried.

'Look,' said Monsieur Felix.

Chandra Lal lay there, his eyes wide open and a thin line of foam on his lips, dead. His body was horribly contorted.

'He's killed himself. We've sent for the doctor. He was too quick for us.'

from *Ashenden* by SOMERSET MAUGHAM

In questions (i) to (x) only one choice is correct.

(i) Ashenden was bitterly disappointed because
A. the woman he loved had failed to answer his letter
B. his plan to get the German Agent to come to Thonon had failed
C. the woman he loved had sent him a letter but it had been intercepted
D. the woman he loved had died

(ii) As Ashenden was walking towards the lake
A. he saw the steamer leaving
B. he saw the German Agent running towards him
C. it began to get light
D. he finished his business

(iii) When he received the letter, Chandra
A. opened it
B. turned it over

C. said he could not understand it because it was in a foreign language
D. turned pale

(iv) When Ashenden reached Chandra, the latter was
A. gesticulating wildly
B. dead
C. killing himself
D. running quickly away

(v) 'he might be a few minutes late' (ll. 16–17) means
A. Felix might be late
B. Chandra might be late
C. Ashenden might be late
D. the agent working in Germany might be late

(vi) 'intercepted' (l. 5) means
A. destroyed
B. lost
C. written
D. got hold of

(vii) 'had an inspiration' (l. 6) means
A. took a deep breath
B. opened the letter
C. had a good idea
D. couldn't think what to do

(viii) 'he quickened his steps' (l. 23) means
A. he walked faster
B. he walked quickly downstairs
C. he quickly stopped
D. he ran away
E. he walked quickly home

(ix) 'panting' (l. 29) means
A. laughing loudly
B. shouting desperately
C. breathing hard
D. running faster

(x) 'he burst into the waiting-room' (l. 45) means
A. he came into the waiting-room and began to laugh
B. he rushed into the waiting-room
C. he knocked down the door of the waiting-room
D. he came into the waiting-room and began to talk in a loud voice

To answer the following, write down the number of the question and the letter of every item that could fill the gap. The items you choose must be grammatically correct and must correspond to the meaning in the original passage.

(xi) He is to say the lady ...... the letter.
A. returned
B. came back
C. sent on
D. turned back
E. replied

(xii) The next boat on which ...... arrived about five.
A. it was possible for Chandra to come
B. it was possible Chandra coming
C. Chandra was possible coming
D. it was possible that Chandra came
E. it was possible that Chandra could come

(xiii) Ashenden told Felix ......
A. that to find the man who had brought the letter
B. to found the man who had brought the letter
C. to find the man who had brought the letter
D. that he should find the man who had brought the letter
E. finding the man who had brought the letter

(xiv) There was no great hurry, ... the train did not start till shortly after eight.
A. until
B. as
C. because
D. therefore
E. since

(xv) Chandra said in French to the man ......
A. 'when did the boat go to Thonon?'
B. 'when was the boat going to Thonon?'
C. 'when would the boat go to Thonon?'
D. 'when does the boat go to Thonon?'
E. 'when the boat goes to Thonon?'

(xvi) When Ashenden reached Chandra he found him ...... on the ground.
A. laying
B. lay
C. to lay
D. to lie
E. lying

(xvii) Ashenden's attempt to ...... Chandra to come to Thonon had failed.
A. make
B. convince
C. persuade
D. allow
E. prevent

(xviii) Describe in not more than 80 words what Chandra did from the moment he received his unopened letter.

3 *On buying books*

Time spent in a bookshop can be most enjoyable, whether you are a book-lover or merely there to buy a book as a present. You may even have entered the shop just to find shelter from a sudden shower. Whatever the reason, you can soon become totally unaware of your surroundings. The desire to pick up a book with an attractive dust-jacket is irresistible, although this method of selection ought not to be followed, as you might end up with a rather dull book. You soon become engrossed in some book or other, and usually it is only much later that you realise you have spent far too much time there and must dash off to keep some forgotten appointment – without buying a book, of course.

This opportunity to escape the realities of everyday life is, I think, the main attraction of a bookshop. There are not many places where it is possible to do this. A music shop is very much like a bookshop. You can wander round such places to your heart's content. If it is a good shop, no assistant will approach you with the inevitable greeting: 'Can I help you, sir?' You needn't buy anything you don't want. In a bookshop an assistant should remain in the background until you have finished browsing. Then, and only then, are his services necessary. Of course, you may want to find out where a particular section is, but when he has led you there, the assistant should retire discreetly and look as if he is not interested in selling a single book.

You have to be careful not to be attracted by the variety of books in a bookshop. It is very easy to enter the shop looking for a book on, say, ancient coins and to come out carrying a copy of the latest best-selling novel and perhaps a book about brass-rubbing – something which had only vaguely interested you up till then. This volume on the subject, however, happened to be so well illustrated and the part of the text you read proved so interesting, that you just had to buy it. This sort of thing can be very dangerous. Apart from running up a huge account, you can waste a great deal of time wandering from section to section. Book-sellers must be both long-suffering and indulgent.

There is a story which well illustrates this. A medical student had to read a text-book which was far too expensive for him to buy. He couldn't obtain it from the library and the only copy he could find was in his bookshop. Every afternoon, therefore, he would go along to the shop and read a little of the book at a time. One day, however, he was dismayed to find the book missing from its usual place and was about to leave when he noticed the owner of the shop beckoning to him. Expecting to be told off, he went towards him. To his surprise, the owner pointed to the book, which was tucked away in a corner. 'I put it there in case anyone was tempted to buy it,' he said, and left the delighted student to continue his reading.

by ROBERT BEST

In questions (i) to (xv) only one choice is correct.

(i) You may spend too much time in a bookshop because
A. the dust-jackets are very attractive
B. you start reading one of the books
C. it is raining outside
D. you have to make sure you don't buy a dull book as a present

(ii) In a good bookshop
A. nobody takes any notice of you
B. the assistant greets you in a friendly way
C. your heart is contented
D. you feel that you are in a music shop

(iii) An assistant should help you
A. as soon as you have entered the shop
B. just before you finish browsing
C. only when you have finished browsing
D. when he leads you to a particular section

(iv) It is very easy to enter a bookshop and buy
A. a book on ancient coins
B. a best-selling novel on brass-rubbing
C. a book that only vaguely interests you
D. a book that unexpectedly interests you

(v) 'There is a story that illustrates this.' (l. 36). 'This' refers to
A. the fact one can be tempted to buy well illustrated books
B. the need for book-sellers to be patient and kind
C. the fact one can waste a lot of time in a bookshop
D. a medical student having to read a text-book which was far too expensive for him to buy

(vi) The text-book the medical student was interested in was tucked away in a corner
A. to prevent anyone from buying it
B. because the medical student might take it away
C. in case the medical student was tempted to buy it
D. because it was a rare and expensive book

(vii) The medical student was surprised because
A. he saw the owner beckoning to him
B. the book wasn't in its usual place
C. he had expected the owner to be angry with him
D. he was about to leave

(viii) Time spent in a bookshop can
A. be very much enjoyed
B. be joyful
C. be greatly enjoying
D. being very pleasant

(ix) 'a sudden shower' (ll. 3–4) means
A. a show of books
B. a downpour
C. a gust of wind
D. the cold

(x) 'might end up with' (l. 7) means
A. come to the end of
B. find yourself the possessor of
C. stop reading
D. put an end to

(xi) 'to your heart's content' (ll. 16–17) means
A. for the good of your health
B. in order to keep happy
C. in the heart of a city
D. for as long as it pleases you

(xii) 'browsing' (l. 20) means
A. buying
B. looking through books
C. falling asleep over a book
D. making lists of books

(xiii) 'so well illustrated' (l. 31) means
A. such a good example
B. having good pictures and diagrams
C. such a fine illustration of the subject
D. so splendid

(xiv) 'running up a huge account' (l. 33) means
A. spending too much time reading lengthy stories
B. ordering books that you are not immediately paying for
C. having to hurry through the rest of the day
D. giving long accounts of your activities

(xv) 'told off' (l. 44) means
A. arrested
B. given special information
C. dismissed
D. reprimanded

To answer the following write down the number of the question and the letter of every item that could fill the gap. The items you choose must be grammatically correct and must correspond to the meaning in the original passage.

(xvi) In a good bookshop you ...... buy anything you don't want.
A. mustn't
B. shouldn't
C. don't have to
D. ought not
E. don't need to

(xvii) The shop assistant should not ask the customer ......
A. if he can be of help
B. if he can help me
C. can I help you
D. if I can help you
E. if he can help him

(xviii) One day he was dismayed to find the book missing and ......, when he noticed the owner beckoning to him.

A. would leave
B. was leaving
C. was just going to leave
D. was on the point of leaving
E. was on leaving
F. should leave

Rewrite the following sentence according to the instruction after it. Change the meaning as little as possible. Change only enough to do what you are asked to and to make a correct sentence.

(xix) 'If it is a good shop, no assistant will approach you with the inevitable greeting "Can I help you, sir?" '
Begin: 'You ......'

(xx) Describe in not more than 80 words what, according to the passage, the disadvantages of being in a bookshop are.

4 *Robbery without violence*

The old lady was glad to be back at the block of flats where she lived. Her shopping had tired her and her basket had grown heavier with every step of the way home. In the lift her thoughts were on lunch and a good rest; but when she got out at her own floor, both were forgotten in her sudden discovery that her front door was open. She was thinking that she must reprimand her daily maid the next morning for such a monstrous piece of negligence, when she remembered that she had gone shopping after the maid had left and she knew that she had turned both keys in their locks. She walked slowly into the hall and at once noticed that all the room doors were open, yet following her regular practice she had shut them before going out. Looking into the drawing room, she saw a scene of confusion over by her writing desk. It was as clear as daylight then that burglars had forced an entry during her absence. Her first impulse was to go round all the rooms looking for the thieves, but then she decided that at her age it might be more prudent to have someone with her, so she went to fetch the porter from his basement. By this time her legs were beginning to tremble, so she sat down and accepted a cup of very strong tea, while he telephoned to the police. Then, her composure regained, she was ready to set off with the porter's assistance to search for any intruders who might still be lurking in her flat.

They went through the rooms, being careful to touch nothing, as they did not want to hinder the police in their search for fingerprints. The chaos was inconceivable. She had lived in the flat for thirty years and was a veritable magpie at hoarding; and it seemed as though everything she possessed had been tossed out and turned over and over. At least sorting out the things she should have discarded years ago was being made easier for her. Then a police inspector arrived with a constable and she told them of her discovery of the ransacked flat. The inspector began to look for fingerprints, while the constable checked that the front door locks had not been forced, thereby proving that the burglars had either used skeleton keys or entered over the balcony. There was no trace of fingerprints, but the inspector found a dirty red bundle that contained jewellery which the old lady said was not hers. So their entry into this flat was apparently not the burglars' first job that day and they must have been disturbed. The inspector then asked the old lady to try to check what was missing by the next day and advised her not to stay alone in the flat for a few nights. The old lady thought he was a fussy creature, but since the porter agreed with him, she rang up her daughter and asked for her help in what she described as a little spot of bother.

from *University of Cambridge Local Examinations Syndicate: Lower Certificate English Composition and Language Paper, June 1962*

In questions (i) to (xii) only one choice is correct.

(i) When she saw the front door was open, she forgot about
A. her basket
B. her keys
C. her lunch
D. her maid

(ii) The old lady was surprised to find the front door open because
A. she had told the maid to shut it
B. she had shut the door herself
C. she saw the maid shut it
D. the maid was not usually negligent

(iii) She realised burglars had been in the flat because
A. she found the front door open
B. the drawing room was in a mess
C. she found the burglars quarrelling among themselves
D. she saw a body by her desk

(iv) She went to see the porter because
A. she was thirsty
B. she didn't want to look at all her rooms alone
C. the porter had a telephone she could use to ring up the police.
D. she very much wanted to tell somebody

(v) The one good thing about the burglars' activity was that
A. it left fingerprints useful to the police
B. it would help the old lady choose things to throw away
C. it showed what the burglars were looking for
D. it indicated how the burglars got into the flat

(vi) The red bundle showed that
A. the burglars used rags to remove their fingerprints
B. the burglars pretended to have work to do so that they could get into houses easily
C. the burglars had stolen things from at least one other house already
D. the burglars were mentally ill

(vii) The porter agreed that
A. it was unwise to remain without company in the flat
B. the inspector was unnecessarily careful
C. the old lady was silly
D. the old lady should ring up her daughter

(viii) 'reprimand' (l. 6) means
A. forgive
B. dismiss
C. tell off
D. ask

(ix) 'prudent' (l. 17) means
A. sensible
B. dangerous
C. pleasant
D. easy

(x) 'tremble' (l. 19) means
A. hurt
B. feel cold
C. shake
D. feel tired

(xi) 'hoarding' (l. 27) means
A. losing things
B. giving things away
C. selling things
D. collecting things

(xii) 'the ransacked flat' (l. 32) means
A. she kept a lot of valuable things in the flat
B. the flat was warm and comfortable
C. someone had gone through the flat looking for valuables
D. the untidy flat

To answer the following, write down the number of the question and the letter of every item that could fill the gap. The items you choose must be grammatically correct and must correspond to the meaning in the original passage.

(xiii) The maid could not have left the doors unlocked ...... she had left the flat first.
- A. as
- B. since
- C. when
- D. after
- E. before

(xiv) The old lady had shut all the doors ...... she usually did.
- A. what
- B. like
- C. as
- D. than
- E. that

(xv) The porter and the old lady set off ...... for any intruders who might still be lurking in the flat.
- A. in search
- B. for searching
- C. on a search
- D. to search
- E. so that they would search

(xvi) Some of the things the burglars had thrown about ...... years before.
- A. would have been discarded
- B. ought to be discarded
- C. should have been discarded
- D. were to discard
- E. were to have been discarded

(xvii) The inspector asked her to ...... what was missing by the next day.
- A. control
- B. investigate
- C. examine
- D. look for
- E. find out

Rewrite the following sentences according to the instructions after each. Change the meaning as little as possible. Change only enough to do what you are asked to and to make a correct sentence.

(xviii) 'They went through the rooms, being careful to touch nothing.'
Begin: 'They were careful ......

(xix) 'The inspector found a dirty red bundle that contained jewellery which the old lady said was not hers.'
Begin: 'The old lady said ......'

(xx) Explain in not more than 80 words what conclusions we can draw from the passage about what the burglars had done.

5 *Escape on bicycles*

I must have dozed off round about dawn, for I was roughly wakened by Morag.

'Be off with you. The car's coming.'

I ran upstairs, dragged Cathleen out of bed, and grabbed my rucksack and we ran to our bikes. We just managed to leave before the car came down the lane.

We came out of a thin wood into open fields, and my heart fell, for there were gates across the path. I fretted at the precious seconds that were lost in opening the first of them – the car was following us. But it was the gates that saved us. It takes longer to open a gate from a car than from a bicycle, and what we gained in this way made up for the extra speed of the car on the stretches between.

It must have looked a preposterous race to an onlooker. I would forge ahead, slide off on to one of the pedals, jump down, and half open the gates. Cathleen following behind would ride through and head for the next gate at full speed. Meanwhile I would slam the gate, making sure it was firmly shut. By the time I reached the next one, Cathleen would have it open and I would ride through and then head for the third, and so on. By this technique we kept the car at bay, a couple of fields behind, and certainly out of shooting range.

At length we came to what I had been hoping for, a stout gate that simply couldn't be opened. I lifted the cycles over. This cost some time – I could see the car catching up. But the great thing was that the car could not be lifted over, and to attempt to force a way through would be to risk damage and delay.

Looking back I saw that we had won. The big car was being slowly turned. We were safe. Soon there would be ample cover near the main road – trees and bushes, in contrast to the open ground we were now crossing.

And so I allowed the pace to slacken. We didn't dawdle by

any means, but travelled at a speed a little more suitable for a tired girl. But this was a mistake.

At first I thought the noise was being made by some farmer at work early. Soon I realized the noise was too loud for only one tractor. When we got to the top of a low hill I realized that four tractors were heading in our direction. They could travel faster than we could over the bumpy ground. The position was plainly desperate. All we could do was abandon our bikes as we could make better time now on foot.

We ran until I thought my lungs would burst, but at every stride the tractors came closer. Next there came a long stretch of rough uphill ground. Everything depended on the other side of the hill. With a great effort we would be ahead when we reached the top. If there were enough bushes on the other side we should be safe.

We arrived at the top. Ahead was a mile of open ground and not a bush or tree in sight. The tractors were certain to run us down.

from *Ossian's Ride* by FRED HOYLE

In questions (i) to (xv) only one choice is correct.

(i) The author and Cathleen were in a hurry because
A. they wanted a lift in a car which was coming along the lane
B. they believed their bicycles had been stolen
C. they would miss the car and be late for work
D. they wanted to escape from the car

(ii) The first gates were not a disadvantage because
A. the car was too big to pass through them
B. they could open them more quickly from a bicycle
C. they allowed the bicycles to go faster on the stretches between
D. they lost precious seconds in opening them

(iii) When they came to a stout gate the author
A. was afraid because it could not be opened
B. was pleased because it couldn't be opened
C. was unhappy because it took a long time to lift the bicycles over it
D. was relieved that the car had been damaged

(iv) The ground they were crossing
A. was covered with trees and bushes

B. hid them
C. had plenty of cover
D. was without any trees or bushes

(v) They travelled more slowly because
A. they didn't dawdle
B. the car was a long way off
C. he believed they were safe
D. he wanted to waste time

(vi) The noise they heard came from
A. a farmer working early
B. a single tractor
C. more than one tractor
D. more than four tractors

(vii) They abandoned their bicycles because
A. the tractors following them were slow
B. they could travel faster without bicycles
C. they couldn't keep their bicycles and ride the tractors at the same time
D. some farmers came to their rescue

(viii) They knew they would be safe if
A. they were still in front at the top of the hill
B. there was cover on the other side of the hill
C. there were not too many bushes on the other side of the hill
D. the tractors could reach them in time

(ix) 'my heart fell' (l. 7) means
A. I felt dismayed
B. my heart beat faster
C. my heart dropped
D. my heart slowed down

(x) 'I fretted' (l. 8) means
A. I was impatient
B. I was angry
C. I was nervous
D. I was frightened

(xi) 'head for' (l. 17) means
A. make for
B. reach
C. get to
D. arrive at

(xii) 'we kept the car at bay' (l. 21) means
A. we stopped the car from catching up with us

B. we made the car stop in a bay
C. we prevented the car from shooting at us
D. we made the car stop a couple of fields behind us

(xiii) 'a stout gate' (ll. 23–24) means
A. a fat gate
B. a brave gate
C. a sturdy gate
D. a vigorous gate

(xiv) 'we could make better time' (ll. 41–42) means
A. we could enjoy ourselves more
B. we could travel more quickly
C. we could travel more comfortably
D. we could gain time

(xv) 'run us down' (ll. 50–51) means
A. give us a lift
B. catch us
C. help us
D. exhaust us

To answer the following, write down the number of the question and the letter of every item that could fill the gap. The items you choose must be grammatically correct and must correspond to the meaning in the original passage

(xvi) I ...... dozed off about dawn, for I was roughly wakened by Morag.
A. suppose I
B. should have
C. would have
D. rightly
E. presumably

(xvii) It does not take as long to open a gate from a bicycle ...... from a car.
A. than
B. that
C. which
D. so
E. as

(xviii) I would slam the gate ......
A. through what Cathleen had just ridden
B. through which Cathleen was just riding
C. that Cathleen had just ridden through
D. which Cathleen just rode through
E. through that Cathleen had just ridden

(xix) That stout gate was ......
A. the thing what I had been hoping for
B. the thing I had been hoping for
C. just what I had been hoping for
D. that what I had been hoping for
E. what I had been hoping for it

(xx) ...... we could do but abandon our bikes.
A. There was nothing
B. It was nothing
C. There was anything
D. It was anything
E. It was not anything

(xxi) ...... a great effort we would be ahead when we reached the top.
A. If making
B. If we should make
C. If we would make
D. If we made
E. Made

(xxii) Describe in not more than 80 words the various things the pursuers did to try and catch the author and Cathleen.

6 *My first job*

While I was waiting to enter university, I saw in a local newspaper a teaching post advertised at a school in a suburb of London about ten miles from where I lived. Being very short of money and wanting to do something useful, I applied, fearing as I did so, that without a degree and with no experience of teaching my chances of landing the job were slim.

However, three days later a letter arrived, summoning me to Croydon for an interview. It proved an awkward journey: a train to Croydon station; a ten-minute bus ride and then a walk of at least a quarter of a mile. As a result I arrived on a hot June morning too depressed to feel nervous.

The school was a dreary, gabled Victorian house of red brick and with big staring sash-windows. The front garden was a gravel square; four evergreen shrubs stood at each corner, where they struggled to survive the dust and fumes from a busy main road.

It was clearly the headmaster himself that opened the door. He was short and rotund. He had a sandy-coloured moustache, a freckled forehead and hardly any hair. He was wearing a tweed suit – one felt somehow he had always worn it – and across his ample stomach was looped a silver watch-chain.

He looked at me with an air of surprised disapproval, as a colonel might look at a private whose bootlaces were undone. 'Ah yes,' he grunted. 'You'd better come inside.' The narrow, sunless hall smelled unpleasantly of stale cabbage: the cream-painted walls had gone a dingy margarine colour, except where they were scarred with ink marks: it was all silent. His study, judging by the crumbs on the carpet, was also his dining-room. On the mantelpiece there was a salt cellar and pepper-pot. 'You'd better sit down,' he said, and proceeded to ask me a number of questions: what subjects had I taken in my General School Certificate; how old was I; what games did I play; then fixing me suddenly with his bloodshot eyes, he asked me whether I thought games were a vital part of a boy's education. I mumbled something about not attaching too much importance to them. He grunted. I had said the wrong thing. The headmaster and I obviously had singularly little in common.

The school, he said, consisted of one class of twenty-four boys, ranging in age from seven to thirteen. I should have to teach all subjects except art, which he taught himself. Football and cricket were played in the Park, a mile away on Wednesday and Saturday afternoons.

The teaching set-up appalled me. I should have to split the class up into three groups and teach them in turn at three different levels; and I was dismayed at the thought of teaching algebra and geometry – two subjects at which I had been completely incompetent at school. Worse perhaps was the idea of Saturday afternoon cricket. It was not so much having to tramp a mile along the dusty streets of Croydon, followed by a crocodile of small boys that I minded, but the fact that most of my friends would be enjoying leisure at that time.

I said diffidently, 'What would my salary be?' 'Twelve pounds a week plus lunch.' Before I could protest, he got to his feet. 'Now', he said, 'you'd better meet my wife. She's the one who really runs this school.'

This was the last straw. I was very young: the prospect of working under a woman constituted the ultimate indignity.

by ROBERT BEST

In questions (i) to (xv) only one choice is correct.

(i) When the writer saw a teaching post advertised in the local paper
A. he was at first afraid to apply for it
B. he applied for it hoping to gain teaching experience
C. he answered the advertisement with little hope of getting the job
D. he applied for the job because the experience might be useful

(ii) The writer did not enjoy the journey because
A. he hated interviews
B. he was nervous
C. it was rather complicated
D. it was too hot to travel comfortably

(iii) The writer thought the headmaster used his study as a dining-room because
A. it smelled of stale cabbage
B. it had margarine on the walls
C. it had cream on the walls
D. it had crumbs on the carpet

(iv) The headmaster looked at the writer disapprovingly
A. as a colonel
B. as an officer might look at a carelessly dressed soldier
C. as if the house was private
D. because his shoes were undone

(v) It was clear to the writer that the headmaster believed that
A. games were unimportant
B. only art was important
C. games were a vital part of a boy's education
D. it was vital for the headmaster and the writer to play the same games

(vi) The writer was unhappy about his teaching programme because
A. there were only two subjects he was competent to teach
B. he only had to teach algebra and geometry
C. he was no good teaching art
D. he was no good at teaching algebra and geometry

(vii) The idea of Saturday afternoon cricket was even worse than teaching because
A. the cricket pitch was a mile away
B. a crocodile of small boys would follow him
C. the streets of Croydon were dusty
D. most of his friends would not be working at that time

(viii) What did he want to do before the headmaster got to his feet?
A. to ask him about his salary
B. to protest about meeting the headmaster's wife
C. to object to having lunch at school
D. to protest at the terms the headmaster offered

(ix) 'landing the job' (l. 6) means
A. taking the job
B. getting the job
C. not getting the job
D. finishing the job

(x) 'awkward' (l. 8) means
A. difficult

B. long
C. depressing
D. short and uninteresting

(xi) 'as a result' (l. 10) means
A. finally
B. consequently
C. in effect
D. in addition

(xii) 'had singularly little in common' (ll. 36–37) means
A. agreed about everything
B. agreed about hardly anything
C. did not have particular interests
D. shared only one interest

(xiii) 'appalled' (l. 43) means
A. appealed to
B. appeared to
C. horrified
D. warned

(xiv) 'at three different levels' (ll. 44–45) means
A. in three separate subjects
B. in three different rooms
C. at three different times
D. at three separate standards

(xv) 'leisure' (l. 51) means
A. pleasure
B. freedom
C. free time
D. hobbies

To answer the following, write down the number of the question and the letter of every item that could fill the gap. The items you choose must be grammatically correct and must correspond to the meaning in the original passage.

(xvi) When I arrived at the school I was so depressed ......
A. that I felt nervous
B. to feel nervous
C. not to feel nervous
D. that I didn't feel nervous
E. because I felt nervous
F. as I felt nervous

(xvii) The headmaster ...... a tweed suit.
A. was dressing

B. was putting on
C. had on
D. was carrying
E. was dressed in
F. was suiting

(xviii) The headmaster told me ...... inside.
A. to come
B. that I came
C. that I had come
D. coming
E. that I should come
F. that I would come

(xix) I ...... taking games on Saturday afternoons.
A. did not want to
B. objected to
C. objected
D. would not
E. looked forward to
F. regretted

(xx) Describe in not more than 80 words what the writer did not like about the job he had applied for.

7 *The hunted*

It must have been the early afternoon when I heard the search-party. As they worked down the slope to the north of my tree I could watch them. The sun was in their eyes, and there was no risk of them spotting my face among the soft green feathers of the larch, which I pushed aside. So far as I could tell, my legs were not bleeding; drops falling on the lower branches would be the only immediate sign of my presence. The slight bloodstains from my hands were there to be seen if anyone looked for them, but, on black boughs in the half-lit centre of a tree, not readily to be seen.

Three uniformed police were trampling down the hillside: heavy, stolid fellows enjoying the sunshine and good-humouredly following a plain-clothes man who was ranging about on my trail like a dog they had taken for a walk. I recognized him as he was the house detective who had conducted the first part of my examination. He had proposed a really obscene method of dragging the truth out of me, and had actually started it when his colleagues protested. They had no objection to his technique, but they had the sense to see that it might be necessary for my corpse to be found and that it must not be found unreasonably mutilated.

Seeing my reptilian trail disappear into the stand of larch, the house detective perked up and took command. He seemed certain that I should be found under the trees so he shouted to his three companions to run round to the other side in case I should escape, and himself crawled under the low boughs. If I were alive the house detective wanted to finish me off discreetly.

He passed rapidly beneath the tree where I was hiding, and on into the open, and I heard him curse when he discovered that I had not stopped in the wood. Then I heard their faint voices as they shouted to one another up and down the stream. That surprised me. I had thought of the stream, naturally, as a morning's march away.

I saw no more of the hunt. A few hours later there was a lot of splashing and excitement down by the water. They must have been dragging the pools for my body. The stream was a shallow mountain torrent, but quite fast enough to roll a man along with it until he was caught by rock or eddy.

In the evening I heard dogs, and felt really frightened. I started to tremble, and knew pain again, aches and stabs and throbbings, all the symphony of pain, all my members fiddling away to the beat of my heart, on it or off it or half a bar behind. I had come back to life, thanks to that healing tree. The dogs might have found me, but their master, whoever he was, never gave them a chance. He wasn't wasting time by putting them on a trail that he could follow himself; he was casting up and down the stream.

When night fell I came down from my tree. I could stand, and, with the aid of two sticks I could shuffle slowly forwards, flat-footed and stiff-legged. I could think, too. None of my mental activities for the past twenty-four hours might be called thinking. I had allowed my body to take charge. It knew far more about escaping and healing than I did.

from *Rogue Male* by GEOFFREY HOUSEHOLD

In questions (i) to (xiii) only one choice is correct.

(i) There was no risk of their spotting the writer's face because
A. they were too far away from the tree
B. the sun wasn't shining on him
C. the leaves of the tree hid him
D. he moved the branches of the tree

(ii) Three uniformed policemen were trampling down the hillside:
A. they had come out to have a walk in the sunshine
B. they were searching for a man wearing plain clothes
C. they were taking a dog for a walk
D. they were hunting for a man who was hiding in a tree

(iii) 'The house detective had proposed a really obscene method of dragging the truth out of him.' His colleagues protested
A. that it would be seen that the writer had been tortured
B. that he was being unnecessarily cruel
C. that he would be punished if the body was discovered
D. that the writer was already unreasonably mutilated

(iv) The house detective shouted to his three companions
A. because he wanted to be alone when he killed the writer
B. because he wanted secretly to help the writer
C. because he wanted to prevent the writer from escaping
D. because he had seen the writer under the trees

(v) What caused the splashing and excitement down by the water?
A. they were dragging the body through the water
B. they were looking for a body in the river
C. a man had been caught between some rocks
D. the water made a lot of noise at this point

(vi) The dogs did not find him
A. because they were being led up and down the stream
B. because the tree had helped him
C. because their master was short of time
D. because their master did not want to give them a chance

(vii) The author had begun to feel better:
A. he was no longer in pain
B. he had been able to have a good rest
C. he had had a swim up and down the stream
D. he was relieved that the dogs had not found him

(viii) He finally came down the tree when
A. he discovered he could walk
B. the pains had gone
C. it was dark
D. he had been up it for twenty-four hours

(ix) 'members' (l. 39) refers to
A. parts of the body
B. noises in the wood
C. policemen
D. fears

(x) 'take charge' (l. 50) means
A. go forward
B. pay the price
C. have control
D. become strong

(xi) 'worked' (l. 2) means
A. laboured hard
B. moved systematically
C. examined quickly
D. dug up the ground

(xii) 'readily' (l. 9) means
A. ready
B. easily
C. intended
D. possible

(xiii) 'finish me off' (l. 25) means
A. complete my interrogation
B. torture me
C. be the one to find me
D. kill me

To answer the following, write down the number of the question and the letter of every item that could fill the gap. The items you choose must be grammatically correct and must correspond to the meaning in the original passage

(xiv) It ...... early afternoon when he heard the search-party.
A. had been
B. might have been
C. was probably
D. ought to have been
E. could be

(xv) He stayed up the tree ...... night.
A. until
B. at
C. throughout the
D. by
E. to

(xvi) The darkness ...... him to remain unseen.
A. made
B. ensured
C. let
D. enabled
E. made possible to

(xvii) He shouted to his three companions to run round to the other side ......
A. in the event I escaped
B. if I happened to escape
C. if I escaped
D. as I might perhaps escape
E. as eventually I would escape

Rewrite the following sentences according to the instructions after each. Change the meaning as little as possible. Change only enough to do what you are asked to do and to make a correct sentence.

(xviii) 'He shouted to his three companions to run round to the other side in case he escaped.'
Begin: 'In order ......'

(xix) 'The dogs might have found me, but their master never gave them a chance.'
Begin: 'The dogs' ......'

(xx) Describe in not more than 80 words the part played by the house detective in the search for the writer.

8 *On the roof of the world*

Late in the afternoon we reached the top of the pass. At last we would be going downhill again. We had finished with wearisome ascents for the time being and glad we were of it. Armin, our yak, however, thought otherwise. He broke away and ran back uphill towards the pass. After endless difficulty we managed to catch him, but we could not get him to move and were obliged to camp in a most inhospitable spot where we could not light a fire – and so we supped on dry meal and raw meat. Our only consolation was the distant view of Mount Everest in the sunset glow.

The next day we tied a rope round Armin's horns and led him over the pass, but he continued to misbehave. We had had enough of Armin and determined to exchange him at the next opportunity for another animal.

Our chance soon came. At the next village I made what I thought was a good bargain and exchanged him for a shaky-looking horse. We were overjoyed and went on our way in high spirits.

On the same day we reached a broad valley through which rushed a stream of green water carrying small ice-floes with it. It was the Tsangpo. That disposed of our dream of finding the river frozen and getting across on the ice. But we did not lose heart. On the opposite bank we saw monasteries and a number of houses and reckoned there must be some means of getting across the river. We thought of a ferry and as we were searching for one I found the piers of a hanging rope bridge. When we came to it we concluded that the bridge was all right for us to cross but no good for our horse. Animals have to swim, though the coolies manage sometimes to carry their donkeys across the swaying rope bridges on their backs. We tried to drive our horse into the water but he simply would not budge. By this time we were quite accustomed to having trouble with our animals, so I sadly made up my mind to go back to the village and try to effect a re-exchange. It cost me money and hard words to get back Armin, but I got him. He showed no sign of pleasure or of sorrow at seeing me again.

It was dark by the time I brought him back to the bridge. By that time it was too late to get him across, so I tied him to a stake nearby. My companion Aufschnaiter had in the meantime found us a lodging and we passed a pleasant, warm night under cover. The villagers were accustomed to passing traders and took little notice of us.

The next morning I forgave Armin all his misdeeds. When we had managed to persuade him to go into the water, he showed himself to be a splendid swimmer.

from *Seven Years in Tibet* by HEINRICH HARRER

In questions (i) to (xii) only one choice is correct.

(i) They had to camp where they could not light a fire because
A. it was a most inhospitable spot
B. they wanted a view of Mount Everest
C. the yak, Armin, would not move
D. they were too tired to go on any further

(ii) They were overjoyed because
A. they had got a lively horse
B. they would soon be able to make a good bargain
C. they had got rid of the yak
D. they had made quite a lot of money

(iii) They thought it must be possible to cross the river because
A. there were buildings on the other side
B. the river was covered with ice
C. they never gave up hope
D. they remembered there was a ferry at that point

(iv) They tried to get the horse into the water because
A. it was essential to teach him to swim
B. only donkeys can walk across rope bridges
C. they were going to use the horse as the ferry
D. they wanted him to swim over the river

(v) As it was dark
A. the author took Armin back to the bridge
B. they spent the night in the village
C. the villagers did not see them very much
D. they were able to sleep well

(vi) The misdeeds which the author forgave Armin were
A. swimming
B. refusing to cross the river
C. making them late the night before
D. his behaviour on the pass

(vii) 'otherwise' (l. 4) means
A. normally
B. in all other cases
C. differently
D. very intelligently

(viii) 'We had had enough of Armin' (ll. 11–12) means
A. Armin had served his purpose
B. we had made as much money as we could expect out of Armin
C. we were tired of Armin
D. we had got enough food from Armin

(ix) 'we did not lose heart' (l. 21) means
A. we did not get cold
B. we did not give up hope
C. we still had a lot of energy
D. we still had feelings

(x) 'budge' (l. 30) means
A. move
B. drink
C. float
D. dive

(xi) 'It cost me hard words' (ll. 32–33) means
A. it was difficult to explain
B. I was ashamed at changing my mind
C. I had to tell lies
D. I had to argue rudely

(xii) 'under cover' (l. 38) means
A. with proper bedclothes
B. with a roof over our heads
C. hidden
D. protected by guards

To answer the following, write down the number of the question and the letter of every item that could fill the gap. The items you choose must be grammatically correct and must correspond to the meaning in the original passage.

(xiii) By this time we ...... trouble.
A. were used to our animals giving
B. used our animals to give
C. got used to our animals
D. had been used to our animals giving
E. had got used to our animals giving

(xiv) I went back to the village to try ...... a re-exchange.
A. to arrange
B. to cause
C. resulting in
D. making
E. to make

(xv) ...... me again Armin showed no sign of pleasure or of sorrow.
A. On seeing
B. By seeing
C. When seeing
D. While seeing
E. To see

(xvi) ...... our search for a ferry I found the piers of a hanging rope bridge.
A. By
B. Meanwhile
C. Within
D. In the course of
E. During

(xvii) ...... in the water Armin showed himself to be a splendid swimmer.
A. Once
B. While
C. Entered
D. Going
E. After

(xviii) We thought there must be ...... we could get across the river.
A. a way
B. some way
C. any way
D. some ways
E. methods

Rewrite the following sentence. Change the meaning as little as possible. Change only enough to do what you are asked to do and to make a correct sentence.

(xix) 'After endless difficulty we managed to catch him, but we could not get him to move and were obliged to camp in a most inhospitable spot where we could not light a fire.'

Begin: 'We were obliged to camp ......', and do not use the word 'because'.

(xx) Imagine you are the yak, Armin. Describe, in not more than 80 words, what you did and what happened to you.

9 *Behind enemy lines*

We were lying up under some trees in the peace of the evening. It looked as though all our dangers were behind us and in a few moments, when the sun set, we would start out on the last stage of our escape to the farm. There had been a strange quietness about the woods all day, yet I knew that after the audacity of our attack in the mine the night before someone would have to swing for it. Our position was still perilous.

Suddenly a dog howled in the village half a mile beneath us in the valley where, barely discernible through the green leaves, were the roofs of farms and clustering outbuildings. Someone said, 'Bloodhounds', and we all laughed, but the next moment they all began to bay together and there were sounds of organised activity. I knew we were in for it then. The light was already beginning to fail; under the canopy of trees it had become quite murky and England seemed far away.

When the silence was first broken by the baying of those bloodhounds, I remember vividly how I felt suddenly sick with fear; my limbs seemed paralysed and I did not trust to the steadiness of my voice to speak. It had been easy to talk of the attractions of defiance and martyrdom back in England, but now to find oneself surrounded in the woods with night coming down and to be hunted remorselessly by one's fellow men seemed terrifying and inhuman. I realised in that moment how dearly one clings to life in the last struggle – instinctively against all reason.

The bloodhounds had clearly got our scent; otherwise they would not have started to track us at that one spot in all those forests, nor would they have begun as night was encroaching. I knew that escape was now beyond us.

At first we sat and listened to that intermittent howling of the dogs, one minute silent and then the next all speaking together like a pack. They sounded at first as if they were veering away from us to the east but then we suddenly heard them again much nearer now in the same part of the woods as we were lurking.

I visualised how any moment men with lanterns following the hounds on the leash would burst into the clearing, and then would follow the last desperate exchange of shots. To be tracked down like criminals and shot in a sweaty suit of clothes was hardly an appealing prospect. I had no wish to flee farther but would have preferred to stand my ground and face our pursuers with what dignity was possible in the sordid circumstances.

But the others were for continuing as long as possible, so I led them off along the forest paths. We made an awful noise on the crackling leaves in our hurry. Once or twice I stopped to listen, for if they were searching the woods for us, they had presumably put a cordon round them.

from *Hugh Dormer's Diaries* (slightly adapted)

In questions (i) to (xv) only one choice is correct.

(i) They were lying up under some trees waiting
A. to make an attack on a mine
B. until all their dangers were behind them
C. for darkness to fall
D. because the woods were peaceful and safe

(ii) The roofs of farms and clustering outbuildings were difficult to see because
A. they were hidden by leaves
B. they were too dark
C. they were too far away
D. they were hidden by the valley

(iii) The author realised how dearly one clings to life in the moment when
A. he felt sick with fear
B. he heard the baying of bloodhounds
C. the light first began to fail
D. his limbs seemed paralysed

(iv) The bloodhounds began tracking them in the dark because
A. it would be more difficult for the men to escape
B. they already knew approximately where they were
C. they hunted better at night
D. the men were too sick to try to escape in the dark

(v) The author led the other men along the forest paths
A. although the author himself did not want to try to escape
B. men were approaching with lanterns and dogs
C. because the sound of the bloodhounds was moving away
D. because they were all desperate to continue as long as possible

(vi) 'someone would have to swing for it' (l. 6) means
A. there would be celebrations later
B. the escape would be made more difficult
C. someone would confess to a mistake
D. someone would have to accept responsibility later

(vii) 'perilous' (l. 7) means
A. frightening
B. dangerous
C. very strange indeed
D. hopeless

(viii) 'clustering' (l. 10) means
A. disused
B. bunched
C. spread out
D. dimly seen

(ix) 'we were in for it' (l. 13) means
A. we were ready
B. we were in a hopeless situation
C. we were about to defend ourselves
D. we were about to be sent to prison again

(x) 'I did not trust the steadiness of my voice to speak' (ll. 18–19) means
A. I had temporarily lost my voice
B. I was afraid my voice might reveal my fear
C. my voice might sound too steady
D. I wasn't sure what I wanted it to say

(xi) 'dearly' (l. 23) means
A. previously
B. hard
C. well
D. expensively

(xii) 'as night was encroaching' (l. 27) means
A. because it was getting dark
B. at night
C. since it was now night
D. with darkness approaching

(xiii) 'prospect' (l. 38) means
A. view
B. suggestion
C. outlook
D. result

(xiv) 'stand my ground' (l. 39) means
A. not sit down
B. move to higher ground
C. insist on having my way
D. remain where I was

(xv) 'they had presumably put a cordon round them' (ll. 44–45) means
A. they had put ropes round the trees
B. they had warned people living nearby
C. they had set up field telephones
D. they had surrounded the woods

To answer the following, write down the number of the question and the letter of every item that could fill the gap. The items you choose must be grammatically correct and must correspond to the meaning in the original passage.

(xvi) The bloodhounds would not have started to track us at that one spot ...... our scent.
A. if they had got
B. otherwise they would had got
C. unless they would have got
D. if they had not got
E. unless they had got
F. unless they had not got

(xvii) ...... the others were for continuing as long as possible I led them off along the forest paths.
A. As
B. Moment
C. Though
D. Although
E. Since
F. For

(xviii) When they heard the bloodhounds night was already beginning ......
A. to fail
B. to set
C. falling

D. to get dark
E. to fall
F. getting dark

(xix) The others ...... as long as possible.
A. were wanting to continue
B. would continue
C. were in favour of continuing
D. wanted to continue
E. were to continue
F. wished continuing

(xx) Describe in not more than 80 words the thoughts that passed through the writer's mind from the moment he first heard the bloodhounds (l. 16), to the time they set off along the forest paths (l. 42).

10 *Boy meets girl*

After we had waited for ten minutes in the crowded tea shop, the clergyman's son came lumbering through the door. My heart leapt and I could feel myself growing pale, my knees under the gingham tablecloth began to tremble. 'There he is,' I whispered. 'Where?' 'There, by the door.' 'You mustn't *wave* to him like that! He'll think you want to see him!' 'Well, I do want to see him!' 'Hush, here he comes.' 'I say, isn't he *tall* ......' She moved up on the oak pew, making room for him.

'Hullo,' I said.

'Hullo,' he said.

We smiled at each other and he clapped his hands together, knocked against a woman at the next table, apologized, at last fitted himself into the pew with his back to Ireen.

'This is Ireen,' I said.

He swivelled round, pulling the tablecloth with him. There was demerara sugar all over the place. He slapped about with a rather dirty handkerchief and Ireen said it didn't matter at all. He then said, 'How do you do?' and held out his big hand which grew out of his rather skimpy sleeve like a beautiful cabbage. She shook it delicately. He then sat on his hands, as though to prevent further damage.

'I've heard so much about you,' Ireen said. Her eyelids were fluttering as mine did when I was trying not to cry. I thought perhaps she had hurt herself in the scuffle. 'It's so nice to meet you at last.'

'Well,' he said. But nothing came after. He was staring at her. Her eyelids beat up and down and for some reason she had clenched the tip of her tongue between her teeth and was smiling at the same time. This gave her the look of a complete maniac. At least two whole minutes went by, while I held my breath and wondered what on earth was happening. Was she having a fit? Was this normal? Should I scream or faint or simply carry on with the conversation?

'Are you going to have an ice-cream?' I said.

'No. No. I can't stop. I can't stay. I've got to ......'

'Oh, but you *must*!' Ireen said, and put her hand on his arm, at the same time impossibly moving her body at least six inches towards him. 'You simply *must* stay!'

Now I knew that in daylight, in public places, the clergyman's son was untouchable. To brush against him by accident was enough to send him crashing away, hair tossing, arms flailing, a fearful embodiment of terror and disgust. Therefore when Ireen assaulted him, so to speak, I drew in my breath, knowing what would happen. He leapt up as though shot, took two steps backwards and overturned a hatstand, whirled round and hit a small child over the head with his great uncontrollable hand, bent sideways, grabbed the hatstand, looked desperately at the screaming child, dropped the hatstand, leapt over the pile of fallen coats straight into a waitress with a tray, turned, gasped, gave a hunted cry and was gone. I let out my breath and took a mouthful of ice-cream. The cafe reassembled itself round me with sounds of protest and distress.

'What a pity,' I said. 'He doesn't like you.'

'Doesn't *like* me?'

'You have to be very careful with some boys,' I said. 'You have to know how to deal with them.'

'If you think he ran away like that because he didn't *like* me——' she shouted, outraged.

I licked my spoon, stroking my tongue with it. 'I know he did.'

from *The Pumpkin Eater* by PENELOPE MORTIMER

In questions (i) to (xv) only one choice is correct.

(i) The clergyman's son came to the tea room
A. to see Ireen and her friend for ten minutes
B. ten minutes after Ireen and her friend
C. after waiting for ten minutes
D. ten minutes before Ireen arrived

(ii) The writer waved to the clergyman's son
A. because the writer wanted to see him
B. when he thought the writer wanted to see him
C. because Ireen didn't know where he was
D. because the writer could only whisper

(iii) He apologized
A. for being nervous
B. for clapping his hands together
C. for accidentally hitting someone
D. for sitting down at the next table

(iv) There was demerara sugar all over the place
A. because every table had lots of sugar
B. because the tablecloth was dirty
C. because the clergyman's son had upset some
D. because he knocked over a bowl of sugar with his handkerchief

(v) When Ireen said it didn't matter she was referring to
A. the clergyman's son's dirty handkerchief
B. the fact that he had sat down at another table
C. the fact that there was demerara sugar all over the table
D. the fact that he was sitting with his back to Ireen

(vi) After the clergyman's son and Ireen had shaken hands he
A. looked like a cabbage
B. sat down
C. sat on his hands
D. damaged his sleeves

(vii) As Ireen put her hand on his arm
A. he said he had to go
B. it was impossible to move
C. she moved nearer to him
D. she was six inches from him

(viii) 'At least two whole minutes went by'. During this time
A. the author stopped herself saying what she wanted to say
B. Ireen had a fit
C. Ireen smiled like a maniac at the clergyman's son
D. the author carried on a desperate conversation

(ix) The clergyman's son leapt up as though shot, because
A. Ireen had touched him
B. Ireen had asked him to stay
C. he didn't like public places in daylight
D. Ireen had hurt him

(x) 'to brush against him by accident' (l. 40) means
A. to meet him by chance
B. to wipe him clean after he had spilled things
C. to say something which hurt him without meaning to
D. to touch him unintentionally

(xi) 'her eyelids were fluttering' (ll. 22–23) means
A. she was trying not to cry
B. her eyes were hurt
C. her eyes were beautiful
D. she was opening and closing her eyes very quickly

(xii) 'complete' (l. 29) means
A. full
B. experienced
C. sincere
D. absolute

(xiii) 'grabbed' (l. 47) means
A. broke
B. fell against
C. put in the right position
D. seized

(xiv) 'straight' (l. 49) means
A. ahead
B. in front
C. right
D. neither to the left nor to the right

(xv) 'was she having a fit?' (l. 31) means
A. was she deciding whether he was suitable for her?
B. was she suddenly so ill she had lost control of herself?
C. was she suited to him?
D. was she behaving in the right way?

To answer the following, write down the number of the question and the letter of every item that could fill the gap. The items you choose must be grammatically correct and must correspond to the meaning in the original passage.

(xvi) I could feel myself ...... pale.
A. being
B. having
C. turning
D. become

(xvii) She moved up on the oak pew ......
A. for creating space
B. to give him room to sit down
C. by giving him room to sit down
D. in order to save space
E. to give him place

(xviii) You ...... know how to deal with them.
A. ought to
B. would
C. need to
D. are to
E. need

(xix) Ten minutes ...... came lumbering through the door.
A. after he
B. passed and he then
C. went by and at least he
D. went by, finally he
E. later he

(xx) Suppose you had been Ireen. Describe in not more than 80 words the clergyman's son's actions from the moment he appeared at the door until the moment he rose to leave.

11 *A winter to remember*

According to the weather men last winter was one of the worst in living memory.

We live in the depths of the country, and my whole family agree that it was certainly a winter we shall never forget. Snow began to fall at round about the beginning of the New Year and continued on and off for approximately ten days.

At first we were all thrilled to see it. It fell silently and relentlessly in large soft flakes until every ugly patch and corner of our rather rambling garden was smoothed over and had become a spotless white canopy. The children soon spoilt its beauty by having snowball fights and leaving their footprints all over it. Hungry birds too, in search of scraps of food made delicate inpressions on its surface. It was now, when the garden was all churned up and of a dirty grey colour, that a severe frost set in, hardening the snow into ugly lumps of grimy concrete. For the next three months the whole countryside lay in a grip of iron.

Every day the birds grew tamer, often waiting hopefully almost on our backdoor step. We fed them with bits of cheese, chopped up meat and any left-overs we had. We also put out bowls of water, which unfortunately within an hour had frozen solid.

Indoors it was pretty cold too. Our central heating system proved both inadequate and unco-operative: inadequate partly because it needed overhauling and partly because the poor state of the doors and most of the windows made a whistling stream of cold air come through; unco-operative because occasionally it simply went on strike. To make matters worse there were tiny holes in the brickwork of many of the rooms. As a result the water pipes froze so that for several weeks our water supply had to be brought in buckets from a nearby farm. We tried to buy a number of oil-stoves to keep these rooms warm, but other people had thought of doing this too – when we called at the village shop the shop-keeper told us she had sold out and that although there were more on order they were unlikely to be delivered until the spring – which of course, was a great comfort.

Throughout January and February and much of March we sat about in our overcoats and warmed ourselves by tramping to and from the farm, lugging buckets of water.

On one occasion the water actually froze before it reached the house, and our youngest son – not the most intelligent of youths – promptly took it all the way back to the farm.

However, one good thing did happen. One of the children dropped a container with a dozen eggs in it. I stooped down furiously to pick up what I thought would be the messy remains only to discover the eggs had come to no harm – they were as solid as if they had been hard-boiled.

Late in March, it finally thawed. Water squirted from pipes in at least half a dozen places. Instead of carting buckets of water into the kitchen from the farm we now brought them in from different parts of the house. Eventually we found a plumber. The plumber undoubtedly saved us from drowning. I have been devoted to plumbers ever since.

by ROBERT BEST

In questions (i) to (xiv) only one choice is correct.

(i) The family agreed with the weather men that
A. last winter was the worst memory of all
B. it was the worst winter ever known
C. it was so bad they would always remember it
D. it was better to live in the country in winter

(ii) The snow did not remain beautiful for very long because
A. the garden was rather untidy
B. a severe frost set in
C. the children had snowball fights in it
D. the birds were hungry

(iii) The result of prolonged frost was to
A. make the concrete grimy
B. make the birds very tame
C. cause the snow to go a grey colour
D. make the birds hopeful

(iv) The central heating did not keep the house warm partly because

A. it had been overhauled
B. it was on strike
C. windows and doors were left open
D. windows and doors were badly-fitting

(v) They could not buy any oil-stoves because
A. the shop-keeper had sold the shop
B. no new oil-stoves had been ordered
C. oil-stoves were not ordered until spring
D. there were no oil-stoves left

(vi) They went to the farm
A. to take buckets of water
B. to keep warm
C. to fetch water
D. to borrow buckets

(vii) 'The good thing' that happened was
A. that they had many eggs
B. they dropped a dozen eggs
C. the eggs, being hard-boiled, didn't break
D. the eggs, being frozen, were not broken

(viii) When the plumber eventually arrived
A. they were drowning
B. he rescued them from the water
C. they were carrying buckets of water back to the farm
D. water was pouring out of the pipes

(ix) 'round about' (l. 5) means
A. roughly
B. everywhere
C. nearby
D. on

(x) 'within an hour' (l. 21) means
A. after about an hour
B. in one hour
C. in less than an hour
D. an hour later

(xi) '...... of course, was a great comfort' (l. 35) means
A. they were pleased
B. was no comfort
C. helped them considerably
D. gave them cause for satisfaction

(xii) 'only to discover' (l. 45) means
A. without discovering that

B. only after discovering
C. and then discovered
D. so as to discover

(xiii) 'eventually' (l. 50) means
A. soon
B. after some time
C. then
D. at the end

(xiv) 'it finally thawed' (l. 47) means
A. the weather got colder finally
B. the snow and ice turned to water at last
C. the pipes dissolved at last
D. it grew lighter in the end

To answer the following, write down the number of the question and the letter of every item that could fill the gap. The items you choose must be grammatically correct and must correspond to the meaning in the original passage.

(xv) ...... last winter was one of the worst in living memory.
A. Following the weather men
B. In the weather men's view
C. To the weather men's view
D. In the weather men's point of view
E. In the weather men's opinion

(xvi) The cold weather continued ...... three months.
A. during
B. since
C. for
D. while
E. within
F. until

(xvii) The poor state of the doors and most of the windows ...... a whistling stream of cold air come through.
A. allowed
B. enabled
C. caused
D. let

(xviii) Our youngest son, ... that the water was frozen, took it back to the farm.
A. seeing
B. on seeing
C. because

D. saw
E. looking
F. thinking

(xix) Other people had thought ...... oil-stoves too.
A. to buy
B. about buying
C. of buying
D. to buying
E. on buying
F. in buying

(xx) Suppose you were the owner of the house. Describe in not more than 80 words, the discomforts in the house and what happened between the time the frost set in and the thaw began. Use your own words as far as possible. Do not include anything that is not in the passage.

12 *The tigress*

The glade was pear-shaped, roughly a hundred yards long and fifty yards wide, with a stagnant pool of rain-water in the centre of it. Deer and other game used this pool as a drinking-place and wallow and, curious to see the tracks round it, I left the path, which skirted the left-hand side of the glade and passed close under a cliff of rock which extended up to the road. As I approached the pool I saw the pug-marks of the tigress in the soft earth at the edge of the water. She had approached the pool from the same direction as I had, and, evidently disturbed by me, had crossed the water and gone into the dense tree and scrub jungle on the right-hand side of the glade. A great chance lost, for had I kept as careful a look-out in front as I had behind I should have seen her before she saw me. However, though I had missed a chance, the advantages were now all on my side and distinctly in my favour.

The tigress had seen me, or she would not have crossed the pool and hurried for shelter, as her tracks showed she had done. Having seen me, she had also seen that I was alone, and watching me from cover as she undoubtedly was, she would assume I was going to the pool to drink as she had done. My movements up to this had been quite natural, and if I could continue to make her think I was unaware of her presence, she would possibly give me a second chance. Stooping down and keeping a very sharp look-out from under my hat, I coughed several times, splashed the water about, and then, moving very slowly and gathering dry sticks on the way, I went to the foot of the steep rock. Here I built a small fire, and putting my back to the rock lit a cigarette. By the time the cigarette had been smoked the fire had burnt out. I then lay down, and pillowing my head on my left arm placed the rifle on the ground with my finger on the trigger.

The rock above me was too steep for any animal to find foot-hold on. I had therefore only my front to guard, and as the heavy cover nowhere approached to within less than twenty yards of my position I was quite safe. I had all this time neither seen nor heard anything; nevertheless, I was convinced that the tigress was watching me. The rim of my hat, while effectually shading my eyes, did not obstruct my vision, and inch by inch I scanned every bit of the jungle within my range of view. There was not a breath of wind blowing, and not a leaf or blade of grass stirred. My men, whom I had instructed to keep close together and sing, from the time they left camp until they joined me on the forest road, were not due for an hour and a half, and during this time it was more than likely that the tigress would break cover and try to stalk or rush me.

from *Man-Eaters of Kumaon* by JIM CORBETT

In questions (i) to (xv) only one choice is correct.

(i) The author left the path because
A. he wanted to see the tracks round it
B. he did not want to disturb the deer and other game which were drinking there
C. he wanted to skirt the left-hand side of the glade
D. he wanted to see the tracks round the pool

(ii) The tigress had gone into the jungle because
A. she had crossed the water
B. she had seen the author coming
C. she had left her pug-marks in the soft earth at the edge of the water
D. she had approached the pool from the same direction as the author

(iii) The author would have seen the tigress before she saw him
A. if he had kept a careful look-out in front and behind
B. had he not crossed the pool and disappeared into the jungle
C. had he kept a careful look-out behind
D. if he had not kept a sufficiently careful look-out in front

(iv) The advantages were now all on the author's side because
A. the tigress had seen him
B. the tigress was watching him from cover
C. the tigress did not realise he knew she was there
D. he was unaware of her presence

(v) The author splashed the water about in order to
A. keep a sharp look-out

B. make the tigress think he was drinking
C. go to the pool to drink
D. move very slowly

(vi) The author lay down as soon as
A. the fire had gone out
B. he had lit a cigarette
C. he had finished his cigarette
D. he had placed the rifle on the ground

(vii) The author had only his front to guard because
A. the heavy cover nowhere approached to within less than twenty yards of his position
B. he was protected by the rock behind him
C. he could see the tigress in front of him
D. he had his rifle with him

(viii) 'roughly' (l. 1) means
A. unevenly
B. rudely
C. about
D. hardly

(ix) 'on the way' (l. 26) means
A. as I went
B. along the road
C. in a way
D. the right way

(x) 'from cover' (l. 19) means
A. hidden in the jungle
B. carefully
C. silently
D. from the cover of the pool

(xi) 'stooping down' (l. 23) means
A. lying down
B. watching the ground
C. bending down
D. looking down

(xii) 'convinced' (l. 35) means
A. frightened
B. sure
C. not sure
D. worried

(xiii) 'obstruct my vision' (l. 37) means did not
A. keep the sun out of my eyes

B. help me to see
C. darken my eyes
D. prevent me from seeing

(xiv) 'scanned' (l. 37) means
A. walked through
B. looked after
C. shot at
D. examined

(xv) 'more than likely' (ll. 42–43) means
A. very probable
B. very probably
C. impossible
D. possible

Rewrite the following sentence. Change the meaning as little as possible. Change only enough to do what you are asked to do and to make a correct sentence.

xvi) 'The tigress had seen me, or she would not have crossed the pool and hurried for shelter, as her tracks showed her to have done.'
Begin: 'The tigress would not have crossed the pool......'

To answer the following, write down the number of the question and the letter of every item that could fill the gap. The items you choose must be grammatically correct and must correspond to the meaning in the original passage.

(xvii) The rock above me was so steep ......
A. that any animal could find a foot-hold on it
B. for any animal to find a foot-hold on
C. for no animal to find a foot-hold on
D. that no animal could find a foot-hold on it
E. that no animal could find a foot-hold on

(xviii) ...... I had neither seen nor heard anything I was convinced that the tigress was watching me.
A. Moreover
B. Although
C. But
D. Though
E. Nevertheless
F. In spite of

(xix) The rim of my hat shaded my eyes ...... my vision.
A. by not obstructing

B. without obstructing
C. by obstructing
D. while not obstructing
E. but did not obstruct
F. while obstructing

(xx) In not more than 80 words, using your own words as far as possible, describe what you think the tigress must have seen from the moment the author approached the pool.

13 Attack on the camp

Landing at Berberah, which was almost empty as it was the season of the Fair, they pitched their tents in a line on the sand, Stroyan on the right, Herne and Burton in the middle, and Speke on the left, and prepared to await a cargo of instruments on their way from Europe. At this moment the gunboat was unfortunately called away, an act which was at once signalled by spies to the hills.

Just before dawn on the 19th of April, the party were awakened by a rush of feet and the screams of the speared and fleeing guards. Burton sprang up and called for his sabre, at the same time sending Herne to ascertain the force of the attack. Herne took a revolver, found that the camp was being assailed by some 200 warriors, shot one who tried to brain him, and returned with the news that the guard had fled and the warriors were massing to attack the tents. Meanwhile Burton had gone to arouse Speke and Stroyan. Speke grabbed a revolver and ran to join Burton in his tent, but Stroyan fell speared in a dozen places before he had gone three yards.

The three remaining officers now crouched in Burton's tent and attempted to make some sort of defence. Burton stood gripping his sabre, while Speke and Herne, with the only pair of available revolvers, blazed at the shadowy figures in the doorway. The attackers meanwhile were running round the tent beating it with clubs, hurling javelins through the walls and tossing their long daggers under the sides. At length when the guy ropes snapped and the canvas threatened to collapse on the beleaguered men, Burton gave the order to sally, leading the way with Herne and Speke at his heels.

A mob met them in the doorway and instinctively gave back before the whirling blade of one of the finest swordsmen in Europe. Seeing what he thought was Stroyan's body lying on the sand, Burton cut his way towards it. At this moment a shout from behind him momentarily made him drop his blade and a spearman leaped in and transfixed him through the cheeks, springing back into the darkness before he could be cut down. Tearing at the firmly embedded weapon and half faint from pain and loss of blood, Burton staggered in search of his comrades, who had disappeared.

Herne's pistol was speedily emptied, but using it as a club he beat his way through the tribesmen, who, though shouting loudly: 'Kill those who are killing us!' for some reason let him pass. Speke, on the other hand, found his pistol jammed and was floored with a blow from a club. Three men bound him and left him to plunder, and he just managed to break free in time to catch the spear of a fourth, who had crept up to slaughter him in his bonds. A succession of thrusts speared the unfortunate man in a dozen places through shoulder, hand, and thigh, and a final stab clean through the right leg made him leap maddened to his feet, dodge a hail of flung spears and totter out of range into the darkness and safety of the town.

from *The Arabian Knight* by SETON DEARDEN

In questions (i) to (xv) only one choice is correct.

(i) When they had landed at Berberah they
A. prepared a cargo of instruments
B. called away the gunboat
C. signalled to spies in the hills
D. set up camp

(ii) Burton sent Herne to
A. take a revolver
B. fetch his sabre
C. find out how many men were attacking them
D. attack the guard

(iii) Burton gave the order to sally because
A. the attackers were tossing their long daggers under the sides of the tent
B. the tent was about to fall and trap them inside
C. the tribesmen had got inside the tent
D. they were outnumbered

(iv) Burton was wounded when
A. he reached Stroyan's body
B. he shouted at someone behind him

C. he was springing into the darkness
D. he was distracted by a shout behind him

(v) After being wounded, Burton
A. fainted from loss of blood
B. dropped his sword
C. went to look for his friends
D. disappeared

(vi) Herne escaped
A. because the tribesmen did not try to stop him
B. by killing all the tribesmen
C. by shooting his way through
D. by shouting loudly

(vii) After his pistol jammed Speke
A. was killed by a blow from a club
B. was tied up
C. seized a spear to defend himself
D. was left to plunder

(viii) 'tried to brain him' (l. 12) means
A. tried to trick him
B. attempted to kill him by hitting him on the head
C. tried to shoot him through the head
D. attempted to spear him

(ix) 'blazed at the shadowy figures' (l. 21) means
A. set fire to the darkened tents
B. made fires so that they could see their attackers
C. got angry because they could not see their attackers properly
D. fired at their attackers, who were difficult to see

(x) 'gave the order to sally' (l. 26) means
A. ordered Sally to lead the way
B. ordered Herne and Speke to break out with him
C. gave Sally an order
D. ordered Herne and Speke to lead the way

(xi) 'gave back' (l. 28) means
A. returned to the attack
B. turned round and ran
C. surrendered
D. retreated

(xii) 'Burton cut his way towards it' (l. 31) means that
A. Burton used his sword to force his way towards Stroyan's body

B. Burton tried to reach Stroyan's body but was cut while doing so
C. in order to reach Stroyan's body Burton had to cut a path through the sand
D. Burton made a path for Stroyan to reach him

(xiii) 'momentarily made him drop his blade' (l. 32) means that
A. his sword fell to the ground but he immediately picked it up again
B. he turned his head for a moment
C. he lowered his sword for a moment
D. he fell to the ground but he immediately got up again

(xiv) 'clean through the right leg' (l. 47) means that
A. the last stab came from a clean spear
B. his right leg was not dirty
C. the last stab passed very close to his right leg
D. a spear went straight through his leg

(xv) 'totter out of range' (l. 48) means
A. run with difficulty to where the spears could no longer reach him
B. run quickly out of sight
C. run from side to side to avoid the spears
D. run like a madman because he was angry

To answer the following, write down the number of the question and the letter of every item that could fill the gap. The items you choose must be grammatically correct and must correspond to the meaning in the original passage.

(xvi) Landing at Berberah they ......
A. put their tents up a line on the sand
B. put in their tents a line on the sand
C. put up their tents in a line on the sand
D. put their tents on a line in the sand
E. put on their tents in a line on the sand

(xvii) Spies signalled to the hills that ......
A. the gunboat was on the way
B. the gunboat had been called away
C. the cargo of instruments was on its way
D. the cargo of instruments had been on its way
E. the gunboat was called away

(xviii) ...... a revolver, Speke ran to join Burton in his tent.
A. Grabbing
B. While grabbing

C. After to have grabbed
D. In grabbing
E. After grabbing
F. By grabbing

(xix) Stroyan ...... by the warriors before he had gone three yards.
A. died
B. killed
C. was killed
D. was dead
E. was killing

(xx) Supposing you were Burton. Describe in not more than 80 words what you did from the moment the attack began.

14 *A tale of war*

Within a matter of minutes Kunze and his section reached the wire in front of the fort. Much of the heavy barbed wire had been torn up by the bombardment, and – with the aid of their pioneer wire-cutters – the section soon made a way through the two entanglements. They reached the spiked railings some fifty yards east of the northern apex of the fort. There was absolutely no way of getting through or over the obstacle. Kunze now followed the railings, moving leftwards, his choice apparently dictated by the machine gun over to his right. He turned the north-east corner and there, just round it, to his delight was a gap about four feet wide that a shell had blasted in the railing. While he was contemplating how to get down into the twenty-four-foot abyss of the moat, Divine Providence made up Kunze's mind for him, in the shape of a near-miss that wafted him over the edge. Temporarily stunned, but otherwise unhurt, Kunze now urged the rest of his section to join him. A corporal, convinced by now that the section leader was out of his mind, announced that he was pulling back, but – possibly persuaded by their own heavy shells which were still falling thickly on the exposed superstructure of the fort – the remainder lowered each other down to where Kunze was standing.

The moat was deserted. Near the breach in the railings were what looked like some small windows and a closed steel door (they were in fact the orifices of the north-east gallery), set high up in the face of the wall. The barrel of a small cannon could be seen protruding from one, so Kunze and his men rapidly took cover as best they could among the debris lying about in the moat. But there was no sign of life here either. Once again, without pausing to consider the possible hazards, Kunze set about getting into the gallery. The steel door, however, was stoutly barred, and the gun embrasures were over twelve feet from the bottom of the moat. Then Kunze suddenly remembered something from the tedious PT exercises of pre-war days. Quickly he ordered his men to form a human pyramid. Several times it collapsed in a tangle of limbs, but eventually Kunze was able to squeeze his body through an embrasure, pushing aside the unmanned revolver-cannon that stood there. The gallery was quite empty. After several efforts, he prised open the steel door, and exhorted his men to climb into it. Faced though with this gaping, tenebrous mouth in the fort exterior, and all the terrible unknown perils that might lie beyond it, Kunze's little troop now began to lose its nerve. Death under one's own shells was infinitely preferable! All but two melted away, abandoning the sergeant in his folly.

from *The Price of Glory: Verdun 1916* by ALISTAIR HORNE

In questions (i) to (xv) only one choice is correct.

(i) Kunze and his men got through the wire by
A. tearing it up
B. cutting it
C. following a road through it
D. bombarding it

(ii) When he reached the railings, Kunze
A. blasted a gap in them
B. was wounded by a machine gun
C. ordered his men to choose a machine gun and go to the right
D. turned to the left

(iii) Kunze got down into the moat by
A. contemplating
B. falling into a hole near the edge
C. being pushed over the edge by a young woman standing nearby
D. being blown over the edge by a shell explosion

(iv) Kunze's men joined him in the moat because
A. he announced he was going to retreat
B. they may have been frightened of being hit by their own guns
C. they fell down into it
D. they were stunned

(v) Kunze and his men took cover because
A. the moat was deserted

B. they were frightened of being shot at
C. there was debris lying about in the moat
D. they saw some small windows and a closed steel door

(vi) Kunze ordered his men to form a human pyramid in order to
A. collapse in a tangle of limbs
B. give them some exercise
C. reach one of the embrasures
D. knock down the steel door

(vii) When Kunze exhorted his men to climb up into the fort
A. they opened their mouths and gaped
B. all but two burst into tears
C. most of them ran away
D. all but two had been killed by their own shells

(viii) 'Divine Providence made up Kunze's mind for him' (l. 13) means
A. religion played a large part in Kunze's life
B. Kunze had an unusual gift for making the right decision
C. Kunze was lucky enough not to have to decide
D. the thought of his girl made Kunze act

(ix) 'out of his mind' (l. 17) means
A. utterly weary
B. mad
C. inspired
D. behaving in a cowardly manner

(x) 'temporarily stunned' (ll. 14–15) means
A. badly hurt
B. knocked out for a moment
C. knocked out for a long time
D. frightened for a moment

(xi) 'pulling back' (ll. 17–18) means
A. taking back
B. dragging back
C. going back
D. carrying back

(xii) 'protruding' (l. 26) means
A. sticking out
B. shooting
C. moving
D. rolling

(xiii) 'took cover' (ll. 26–27) means
A. put on more clothes
B. took off their hats
C. hid
D. picked up pieces of the debris and used them to cover themselves

(xiv) 'unmanned' (l. 36) means that
A. the revolver-cannon was damaged
B. there was no one working the revolver-cannon
C. the revolver-cannon was in pieces
D. the revolver-cannon had no ammunition

(xv) 'lose its nerve' (l. 40) means
A. get into a rage
B. grow calm
C. go mad
D. become very frightened

To answer the following, write down the number of the questions and the letter of every item that could fill the gap. The items you choose must be grammatically correct and must correspond to the meaning in the original passage.

(xvi) ...... Kunze and his section a matter of minutes to reach the wire in front of the fort.
A. There was
B. It needed
C. It took
D. It lasted
E. It was necessary

(xvii) ...... to get through or over the spiked railings.
A. It was absolutely unable
B. There was absolutely no possibility
C. It was absolutely no possibility
D. It was absolutely impossible
E. There was absolutely impossible

(xviii) A corporal was ...... that the section leader was out of his mind.
A. sure
B. knowing
C. wondering
D. persuaded
E. considered
F. certain

(xix) The ...... men lowered each other down to where Kunze was standing.

A. resting
B. remains of the
C. rest of the
D. remaining
E. rest

(xx) Describe in not more than 80 words how Kunze and his men overcame the various obstacles which they encountered.

15 Disaster in the air

I settled down in Ferguson's armchair to read the report upon the accident to the prototype Reindeer.

It had flown from London Airport on the night of March 27th with a crew of nine and a passenger list of twenty-two persons, including the Russian Ambassador to Ottawa, thirty-one people in all. It had been diverted from Gander on account of fog and had landed at Goose at about 7 a.m. G.M.T. on the morning of the 28th. It had refuelled there, and had taken off for Montreal at 9.17 in weather that was overcast and raining: the temperature was above freezing, unusual for the time of year. The crew had not reported any trouble at Goose. One wireless message of a routine character was received at 9.46 reporting that the aircraft was on course at 16,500 feet. That was the last that was heard of it.

It was three days before it was reported by one of the search aircraft, though the spot where it was finally located had been flown over several times. It was another two days before a party succeeded in getting to the wreckage. They flew up in a Norseman fitted with skis and landed in deep snow on a frozen lake called Small Pine Water: the landing was a hazardous one because of the alternate thaw and freeze: the skis mushed in beneath the icy crust. The party then had to force their way eleven miles over the snow-covered hills, thickly covered with a forest of spruce and alder. The night temperatures were as low as – 45° Fahrenheit, making it a most difficult search: several of the party suffered from frostbite. In the deep snow and the forest growth they would never have found the crash at all but for the continuous guidance given by the aircraft working with them.

In the circumstances, it is hardly surprising that their investigation was, in some respects, perfunctory.

The spot where the Reindeer crashed was about 250 miles from Goose, about 50 miles west of the Moisie river and about 100 miles north of the sea coast in the Gulf of St. Lawrence. It was just in Canada, in the Province of Quebec.

The bulk of the aircraft was found lying in deep snow among trees at the foot of a cliff, the estimated height of which was 340 feet. It had been on fire after the crash and everything in it was totally destroyed. All the bodies were found within the flattened shell of the fuselage, indicating that nobody had survived the accident. The cliff face at that point ran approximately east and west along the aircraft's course, and the Reindeer had hit first at the top of this cliff, very near the edge. It had knocked down three trees, and here the starboard wing had been torn off; the wing was found at some distance from the rest of the machine, at the foot of the cliff. Two propeller blades and portions of the engine cowling were found on top of the cliff. The fuselage had then toppled over the cliff and had crashed down into the forest below, and burnt out.

From the damage to the trees it seemed that the original impact, the first touch, had been with the machine at a small angle of descent, probably not more than ten degrees below the horizontal. From that the investigators had deduced that the machine was under control up to the moment of impact, and from that, that the pilot had been deliberately losing height through the clouds in order to check his position by a sight of the ground.

from *No Highway* by NEVIL SHUTE

In questions (i) to (xv) only one choice is correct.

(i) The Russian Ambassador
A. was travelling from London
B. left Ottawa
C. went to Russia
D. arrived in Ottawa

(ii) The time between when the aircraft crashed and when it was known where it had crashed was
A. one day
B. two days
C. three days
D. five days

(iii) After leaving London Airport the Reindeer aircraft
A. arrived at Montreal at 9.17
B. set off for Gander

C. set off for Goose
D. landed at Gander and set off for Montreal

(iv) One reason for the difficulty the search party had in finding the crash was that
A. the forest was expanding
B. the forest was so big it was difficult to find their way out of it
C. there was thick vegetation
D. the trees were too tall

(v) The search-party were able to find the crashed aircraft because
A. they were using a sledge fitted with skis
B. they flew to the spot in several aircraft
C. an aircraft led them to it
D. they were able to land on a lake

(vi) The first thing the aircraft hit was
A. the cliff face
B. the foot of the cliff
C. some trees
D. the forest below the cliff

(vii) The investigators thought that the moment before the accident the pilot
A. was flying above the cloud
B. was flying too low
C. moved from where he was sitting when he saw the ground
D. did not have sufficient control of the machine

(viii) 'of a routine character' (ll. 11–12) means
A. about a regular passenger
B. about an airline time-table
C. of a boring nature
D. about normal matters

(ix) 'on course' (l. 13) means
A. naturally
B. at its normal height
C. doing safety-drill in case of trouble
D. heading in the right direction

(x) 'located' (l. 15) means
A. found
B. placed
C. fixed
D. taken

(xi) 'hardly' (l. 28) means
A. very
B. unfortunately
C. scarcely
D. almost

(xii) 'perfunctory' (l. 29) means
A. appropriate
B. adequate
C. not thorough
D. not correct

(xiii) 'burnt out' (l. 47) means
A. exploded
B. was burnt completely
C. burnt on the outside part
D. set light to the forest

(xiv) 'at a small angle of descent' (ll. 49–50) means
A. diving very steeply
B. just below the edge of the cliff
C. not coming down very steeply
D. turning slightly as it came down

(xv) 'deliberately' (l. 53) means
A. carefully
B. thoughtfully
C. hesitatingly
D. intentionally

To answer the following, write down the number of the question and the letter of every item that would fill the gap. The items you choose must be grammatically correct and must correspond to the meaning in the original passage.

(xvi) The plane had been diverted from Gander ...... fog.
A. because of
B. because
C. in spite of
D. owing to
E. due to
F. for

(xvii) ...... three days the wreck of the plane was reported by one of the search aircraft.
A. Before
B. Until
C. For

D. After
E. During

(xviii) The investigators had deduced that the aircraft ...... under control up to the moment of impact.
A. should have been
B. must have been
C. ought to have been
D. had been
E. was to be

(xix) The very low night temperatures ...... the search extremely difficult.
A. made
B. caused
C. rendered
D. froze
E. hindered
F. making

(xx) Explain in not more than 80 words what the Reindeer aircraft was thought to have done when it crashed, starting from when it came down through the clouds. Describe the events in the same order as they took place.

16 *Alone at sea*

Niall laughed and stretched himself and yawned. He wondered if it would be a good idea to finish the brandy and the ginger syrup. He stared idly down into the cabin. It was then he noticed, for the first time, the long trickle of water on the cabin floor. He stared at it, puzzled. There was nothing to upset. No spray had come in through the ports; and, anyway, the ports were closed. No rain had settled in the bilges, because no rain had fallen for the past two days. Why then the water on the cabin floor? Niall went down below to inspect the trickle closer.

He put his fingers in the liquid. It was salt. He looked about him for a screw-driver to lift up the floor-board. He found one at last at the back of a locker. The search had taken time, and when he knelt down to lift the board, the trickle had become a stream.

He jerked up the board with his screw-driver, and he saw that the bilges were full of water, salt like the stream upon the floor. In some part of the boat, whether forward or aft he had no notion where, a leak had sprung. He supposed that it must be a bad leak because of the rate at which the water was entering the boat.

He wondered what to do. He took up more floor-boards, with the idea of finding the leak and plugging it with something, but when he did this the water came up more quickly and lapped over his feet.

He hastily put back the boards, so that the water became a stream again. But the trouble was that it became an ever-widening stream.

He remembered vaguely a phrase from boyhood books, 'All hands to the pumps,' and he knew there was a pump in the locker aft of the cockpit. He found the pump. It was rusty, he had not used it for some time. He assembled it clumsily and placed the nozzle in the socket on the deck. It made a curious hissing sound like the pump on a child's bicycle that would not work. It felt much too light. He took it out of the nozzle and examined it. The rubber washer round the base had perished, and there was a hole that should have a screw inside it, but the screw was missing. The pump, in fact, was useless. Nor had he a baler; he had left the baler in the dinghy at the moorings. There was an old jug below that would have to serve instead. He went below again to get the jug, but by now the water covered the boards of the floor. He started baling the water with the jug. After five minutes of this, kneeling, with cramped back, and throwing the water from the porthole, he realized that he was making little or no impression on the rising stream. To bale was wasted effort. He went up again on deck.

The wind, if anything, had lightened; the sea was slaty smooth. There was no steamer smoke now on the horizon, and no sign of any ship. The land lay astern, about seven miles distant. Even the gull had gone. Niall sat down in the cockpit once again and watched the water rising on the cabin floor.

from *The Parasites* by DAPHNE DU MAURIER

In questions (i) to (xv) only one choice is correct.

(i) Niall first noticed the water on the cabin floor as he
A. laughed
B. finished the brandy and ginger syrup
C. looked down
D. stretched himself and yawned

(ii) When he found there was water on the cabin floor
A. he was upset
B. he realised rain had come in through the cabin windows
C. he went and tasted it
D. he closed the ports

(iii) It took time
A. to lift the floor-boards
B. to find where the water was coming from
C. to open the locker
D. to find a screw-driver

(iv) He thought the boat was leaking badly because
A. the water was coming in fast
B. the bilges had water in them
C. it was full of salt
D. salt water was coming in forward and aft

(v) He put the floor-boards back as quickly as he could
A. to allow the water to become a stream
B. because he had found the leak
C. having plugged the leak
D. to stop the water coming in so quickly

(vi) When he found the pump
A. he put the various pieces together
B. it was making a curious hissing noise
C. he thought at first it was a child's bicycle pump
D. he realised it was too rusty to use

(vii) Having discovered the pump was useless
A. he used a baler in the dinghy
B. he wanted to use a jug but couldn't reach it
C. he fetched a jug
D. he used his hands to throw the water through the port-hole

(viii) He stopped baling out
A. when his back began to hurt him
B. because he couldn't kneel down any longer
C. because water was entering the boat as fast as he was baling it out
D. when he got the impression that the water was no longer rising

(ix) 'puzzled' (l. 5) means
A. he looked closely at it
B. he couldn't understand where it had come from
C. he was frightened
D. he stood without moving

(x) 'there was nothing to upset' (l. 5) means
A. there was no cause for alarm
B. nothing worried him
C. there was nothing that could have been spilt on the floor
D. there was nothing that could turn anything over

(xi) 'a screw-driver' (l. 11) is
A. a tool
B. a small engine
C. a life-saving device
D. a scientific instrument

(xii) 'notion' (l. 16) is
A. imagination
B. an idea

C. information
D. a memory

(xiii) 'he assembled it clumsily' (l. 29) means
A. fixed it carefully
B. put it in position carelessly
C. put it together unskilfully
D. had difficulty getting it to work

(xiv) 'the rubber washer had perished' (ll. 33–34) means
A. it had disappeared
B. it had become rotten
C. it was round at the base
D. it had a hole in it

(xv) 'had lightened' (l. 44) means
A. had become less strong
B. had become less heavy
C. had become less dark
D. had become less smoky

To answer the following, write down the number of the question and the letter of every item that could fill the gap. The items you choose must be grammatically correct and must correspond to the meaning in the original passage.

(xvi) No spray had come in through the ports; ......, the ports were closed.
A. besides
B. beside
C. in any case
D. at any rate
E. no matter

(xvii) The rate at which the water was coming in ...... a bad leak.
A. suggested him
B. told
C. indicated
D. suggested
E. told him

(xviii) He hastily put back the boards, ... a stream again.
A. in order that the water became
B. for making the water into
C. so as the water became
D. by making the water
E. and made the water into

(xix) ......, the pump was useless.
A. As a matter of fact
B. It was a fact
C. The fact was
D. Factually
E. Actually

(xx) Describe in not more than 80 words what Niall did from the moment he wondered what to do (l. 19) to the time he returned on deck (l. 43).

17 *Escape from a prison camp*

The drop to the roof was in full view of a sentry about fifty yards away, who could play a searchlight at will on any desired spot. I dropped quietly and quickly to the flat roof as the sentry's foot-beats indicated his back was turned. I had stockings on my feet, old stockings cut out as mittens on my hands, and a borrowed balaclava helmet concealing the greater part of my face. All was well. Once on the flat roof I was hidden from view and I continued to the higher sloping roof, which ran at right angles to the flat one. I had just succeeded, making a certain amount of noise, in climbing the five feet to the gutter in full view of a second sentry but helped by a shadow, when a commotion began among the guards, a running hither and thither with torches flashing and orders shouted. I lay like a dead thing, spread-eagled on the roof. The commotion increased, but it did not approach the quarter where I was. At midnight a continuous sound of murmuring voices broke out in the most distant of the four courtyards and, after listening for some time, I decided that the noise must be due to the arrival of another group of prisoners. I continued with a lighter heart, for though the noise was far off, it would help me. As I moved, slates cracked like pistol-shots, so it seemed to me, and broken pieces slid down to the edge of the roof with a long-drawn-out rattle. I had to cross over the ridge of the roof, because on the near side I was visible as soon as I left the gable end. On the far side I was out of sight and in deep shadow. I tried to spread my weight as evenly as possible and found the best way to move was to lie on my back with arms and legs stretched out and move slowly sideways. The roof was forty yards long and the drop to the ground was sixty feet. One piece of luck that came my way on this long stretch of the journey was a roof walkway for chimney-sweeps running about half the length, but even this made the most terrifying creaks and groans. It frightened the wits out of me, especially when a loose plank fell right off and slid, rattling loudly, down to the edge. I watched, transfixed with horror, waiting for the moment when it would topple over, and then it stopped, wedged in the gutter.

from *The Colditz Story* by P. R. REID

In questions (i) to (xii) only one choice is correct.

(i) The drop to the roof was dangerous because
A. it was about fifty yards to the roof
B. it was dark and the author could not see what he was doing
C. it could easily be seen by a sentry
D. the author had no shoes on and so might hurt his feet on landing

(ii) The sentry did not see the author drop to the flat roof because
A. the roof was hidden from view
B. he was walking in the opposite direction at the time
C. the author's face was concealed by his helmet
D. he was playing with his searchlight instead of watching the roof

(iii) On reaching the flat roof the author
A. put stockings on his feet
B. hid his face
C. ran to the next roof
D. started to climb up to the next roof

(iv) The author had just reached the gutter, when
A. a second sentry saw him
B. he was shot dead
C. he made a certain amount of noise
D. he heard a lot of noise

(v) At midnight the author
A. heard the voices of the guards searching for him
B. saw some more prisoners arrive
C. reached the fourth courtyard
D. heard a noise in the distance

(vi) As the author moved along the roof
A. the guards seemed to be shooting at him
B. he slid down to the edge and almost fell
C. he fired off a number of pistol-shots
D. pieces of the roof broke off and slid down to the edge

(vii) The author crossed the roof
A. because he didn't want to be seen
B. because it was easier to move on the other side
C. because he wanted to lie on his back
D. so as to be able to use the roof walkway

(viii) The disadvantage of the roof walkway was that
A. it was used by chimney-sweeps
B. it only ran half the length of the roof
C. it was difficult to walk along it
D. it made a lot of noise

(ix) The author was transfixed with horror because
A. he had almost fallen
B. the guards would be sure to hear the plank fall
C. the plank stopped in the gutter
D. he was on the point of falling

(x) 'broke out' (l. 16) means
A. grew louder
B. stopped
C. began
D. got further and further away

(xi) 'with a lighter heart' (l. 19) means
A. feeling happier
B. walking less heavily
C. using a lighter to see where he was going
D. towards the centre of the roof, where it was lighter

(xii) 'loose' (l. 32) means
A. heavy
B. unnoticed
C. big
D. not fixed

To answer the following, write down the number of the question and the letter of every item that could fill the gap. The items you choose must be grammatically correct and correspond to the meaning in the original passage.

(xiii) Once on the flat roof the author was ...... the sentry.
A. not seeing
B. impossible to see
C. unseen
D. out of sight of
E. within sight of

(xiv) The author ...... climb the five feet to the gutter.
A. succeeded to
B. managed to
C. finished to
D. enabled to
E. reached to

(xv) ...... the commotion increased, it did not approach the quarter where the author was.
A. But
B. Though
C. However
D. In spite of
E. Although

(xvi) The author decided that the ...... the noise was the arrival of another group of prisoners.
A. cause of
B. reason of
C. result of
D. reason why
E. reason for

(xvii) The author moved along the roof ...... on his back.
A. laying
B. lain
C. lied
D. lying
E. laid

(xviii) The roof was forty yards ......
A. in long
B. of length
C. in length
D. along

(xix) The author ...... topple over.
A. hoped the plank would
B. expected the plank to
C. waited the plank to
D. frightened the plank to
E. was afraid the plank would

(xx) Give an account, in not more than 80 words, of each of the difficulties and dangers that the author encountered in the course of his attempt to escape.

18 *Atlantic convoy*

When the alarm bell went, just before midnight, Ferraby left the bridge where he had been keeping the first watch with Baker, and made his way aft towards his depth-charges. It was he who had rung the bell, as soon as the noise of aircraft and a burst of tracer bullets from the far side of the convoy indicated an attack; but though he had been prepared for the violent clanging and the drumming of feet that followed it, he could not control a feeling of sick surprise at the urgency which now possessed the ship, in its first alarm for action. The night was calm, with a bright three-quarter moon which bathed the upper deck in a cold glow, and showed them the nearest ships of the convoy in hard revealing outline; it was a perfect night for what he knew was coming, and to hurry down the length of *Compass Rose* was like going swiftly to the scaffold. He knew that if he spoke now there would be a tremble in his voice, he knew that full daylight would have shown his face pale and his lips shaking; he knew that he was not really ready for this moment, in spite of the months of training and the gradually sharpening tension. But the moment was here, and somehow it had to be faced.

The attacking aircraft was now flying low over the centre of the convoy, pursued and harried by gun-fire from scores of ships at once. The plane could not be seen, but her swift progress could be followed by the glowing arcs of tracer-bullets which swept like a huge fan across the top of the convoy. The uproar was prodigious – the plane screaming through the darkness, hundreds of guns going at once, one or two ships sounding the alarm on their sirens: the centre of the convoy, with everyone blazing away at the low-flying plane and not worrying about what else was in the line of fire, must have been an inferno. Standing in their groups aft, close to the hurrying water, they watched and waited, wondering which way the plane would turn at the end of her run: on the platform above them the two-pounder gun's crew, motionless and helmeted against the night sky, were keyed ready for their chance to fire. But the chance never came, the waiting belts of ammunition remained idle: something else forestalled them.

It was as if the monstrous noise from the convoy must have a climax, and the climax could only be violent. At the top of the centre column, near the end of her run, the aircraft dropped two bombs: one of them fell wide, raising a huge pluming spout of water which glittered in the moonlight, and the other found its mark. It dropped with an iron clang on some ship which they could not see – and they knew that now they would never see her: for after the first explosion there was a second one, a huge orange flash which lit the whole convoy and the whole sky at one ghastly stroke. The ship – whatever size she was – must have disintegrated on the instant; they were left with the evidence of the sickening succession of splashes as the torn pieces of the ship fell back into the sea, covering and fouling a mile-wide circle, and the noise of the aircraft disappearing into the darkness, a receding tail of sound to underline this fearful destruction.

from *The Cruel Sea* by NICHOLAS MONSERRAT

In questions (i) to (xv) only one choice is correct.

(i) Ferraby left the bridge
A. after he had rung the alarm bell
B. to warn Baker to ring the alarm bell
C. when midnight struck
D. when he heard the sound of the depth-charges

(ii) It was a perfect night
A. to watch the convoy in the moonlight
B. to attack ships in convoy
C. to attack an aircraft
D. to bathe on the upper deck

(iii) If it had been full day-light
A. he would have been prepared for this moment
B. he would have been able to face the danger
C. people would have seen he looked frightened
D. they would have been less frightened

(iv) Scores of ships
A. sailed in pursuit of the plane

B. were struck by tracer-bullets
C. fired at the aircraft
D. were fired at by the aircraft

(v) The centre of the convoy was a terrible place to be because
A. of the screaming of the aircraft
B. the aircraft might crash there
C. the ships might hit each other with their gunfire
D. of the heat from the firing guns

(vi) The two-pounder gun's crew
A. wandered about on the platform
B. fired at the aircraft
C. waited with excitement to fire their gun
D. watched the plane turn in the night sky

(vii) The second of the two bombs
A. struck the water
B. hit a ship
C. exploded in an orange flame
D. glittered in the moonlight

(viii) The 'evidence' they were left with refers to
A. the parts of the ship that were falling into the sea
B. the size of the ship
C. the wreck of the aircraft
D. the destruction of the entire convoy

(ix) 'the glowing arcs of tracer-bullets' (l. 23)
A. showed up the plane
B. were aimed at the convoy
C. showed the plane's course
D. helped the plane to follow the convoy

(x) 'keeping the ...... watch' (l. 2) means
A. looking
B. keeping an eye on your watch
C. being on duty
D. seeing what time it was

(xi) 'possessed' (l. 8) means
A. owned
B. dominated
C. had
D. belonged to

(xii) 'hard' (l. 11) means
A. almost

B. hardly
C. clear
D. difficult

(xiii) 'hurry down the length' (l. 13) means
A. go swiftly from one end of the ship to the other
B. reduce speed quickly
C. descend the ladder from one deck to another at speed
D. take cover as fast as possible

(xiv) 'blazing away' (l. 28) means
A. on fire
B. firing guns furiously
C. shouting with excitement
D. rushing off in panic

(xv) 'receding' (l. 50) means
A. back
B. broken
C. going away
D. getting louder

To answer the following, write down the number of each question and the letter of every item that could fill the gap. The items you choose must be grammatically correct and must correspond to the meaning in the original passage.

(xvi) The noise of aircraft warned Ferraby ......
A. the coming attack
B. the attack was coming
C. of the coming attack
D. of the attack that was coming
E. to the coming attack
F. that the attack came

(xvii) If Ferraby ...... a tremble in his voice.
A. had spoken, there had been
B. would have spoken, there would have been
C. would speak, there would be
D. had spoken, there should have been
E. had spoken, there would have been

(xviii) It was a perfect night for ...... he knew was coming.
A. that
B. which
C. that which
D. whatever
E. whom

(xix) The second bomb ...... a ship.
A. struck
B. bombed
C. hit
D. marked
E. crashed
F. hurt

(xx) In not more than 80 words, and using your own as far as possible, describe what was heard from *Compass Rose* from the moment the aircraft flew low over the convoy (l. 20).

19 A dog called Muggs

The Airedale's name was Muggs, and he was, as I have said, the worst of all my dogs. A big, burly, choleric dog, he always acted as if he thought I wasn't one of the family. There was a slight advantage in being one of the family, for he didn't bite the family as often as he bit strangers.

One morning when Muggs bit me slightly, more or less in passing, I reached down and grabbed his short stumpy tail and hoisted him into the air. It was a foolhardy thing to do. As long as I held the dog off the floor by his tail he couldn't get at me, but he twisted and jerked so, snarling all the time, that I realised I couldn't hold him that way very long. I carried him to the kitchen and flung him on to the floor and shut the door on him just as he crashed against it. But I forgot about the backstairs. Muggs went up the backstairs and down the frontstairs and had me cornered in the living-room. I managed to get up on to the mantelpiece above the fireplace, but it gave way and came down with a tremendous crash, throwing a large marble clock, several vases, and myself heavily to the floor. Muggs was so alarmed by the racket that when I picked myself up he had disappeared.

In his last years Muggs used to spend practically all of his time outdoors. He didn't like to stay in the house for some reason or other – perhaps it held too many unpleasant memories for him. Anyway, it was hard to get him to come in, and as a result the garbage man, the iceman, and the laundryman wouldn't come near the house. We had to haul the garbage down to the corner, take the laundry out and bring it back, and meet the iceman a block from home. After this had gone on for some time we hit on an ingenious arrangement for getting the dog into the house so that we could lock him up while the gas-meter was read, and so on. Muggs was afraid of only one thing, an electrical storm. Thunder and lightning frightened him out of his senses (I think he thought a storm had broken the day the mantelpiece fell.) He would rush into the house and hide under a bed or in a clothes closet. So we fixed up a thunder machine out of a long narrow piece of sheet iron with a wooden handle on one end. Mother would shake this vigorously when she wanted to get Muggs into the house. It made an excellent imitation of thunder, but I suppose it was the most roundabout system for running a household that was ever devised. It took a lot out of Mother.

A few months before Muggs died, he got to 'seeing things'. He would rise slowly from the floor, growling low, and stalk stiff-legged and menacing toward nothing at all. Sometimes the Thing would be just a little to the right or left of a visitor. Once a Fuller Brush salesman got hysterics. Muggs came wandering into the room like Hamlet following his father's ghost. His eyes were fixed on a spot just to the left of the salesman, who stood it until Muggs was about three slow, creeping paces from him. Then he shouted. Muggs wavered on past him into the hallway, grumbling to himself, but the salesman went on shouting. Mother had to throw a saucepan of cold water on him before he stopped. That was the way she used to stop us boys when we got into fights.

Muggs died quite suddenly one night. We buried him beside a lonely road with a smooth board above his grave. On it I wrote with an indelible pencil 'Cave Canem'. Mother was quite pleased with the simple classic dignity of the old Latin epitaph.

from *The Dog That Bit People* by JAMES THURBER (adapted)

In questions (i) to (xii) only one choice is correct.

(i) If you were a member of the family, the 'slight advantage' was that
A. you were only bitten slightly
B. you were not bitten in as many places as strangers were
C. you were bitten less frequently than strangers were
D. you were bitten less severely than strangers were

(ii) The garbage man wouldn't come near, because
A. Muggs had too many unpleasant memories
B. Muggs had a reason for staying in the house
C. They hauled the garbage down to the corner
D. Muggs was loose

(iii) The Fuller Brush salesman got hysterics, because
A. the Thing was just to the left of him

B. Mother threw cold water on him
C. Muggs walked stiff-legged toward him
D. he stood on the same spot too long

(iv) The thunder machine was made in order to
A. make it easier for mother to run about in the house
B. make Muggs come into the house
C. get Mother to give things away
D. get Muggs used to electrical storms

(v) 'Muggs bit me slightly' (l. 6) means Muggs
A. bit me by mistake
B. seldom bit me
C. gave me a little bite
D. gave me an occasional bite

(vi) 'it gave way' (l. 16) means
A. it was a place where one could walk
B. solved the problem
C. allowed Muggs to reach the author
D. broke under the author's weight

(vii) 'It took a lot out of Mother' (l. 39) means
A. it tired her a lot
B. it cost her a lot of money
C. it made her lose weight
D. it took her a lot of time

(viii) 'hit on' (l. 27) means
A. found hidden somewhere in the house
B. nailed together
C. agreed on
D. thought of

(ix) 'practically' (l. 20) means
A. in practice
B. nearly
C. taking exercise
D. conveniently

(x) 'wouldn't' (l. 24) means
A. usually didn't
B. refused to
C. hadn't to
D. disliked

(xi) 'racket' (l. 19) means
A. things that had fallen on him

B. injury
C. damage
D. noise

(xii) 'would rush' (l. 33) means
A. might have rushed
B. wanted to rush
C. preferred to rush
D. used to rush

To answer the following, write down the number of the question and the letter of every item that could fill the gap. The items you choose must be grammatically correct and must correspond to the meaning in the original passage.

(xiii) The dog couldn't get at me ...... I held him up.
A. in case
B. while
C. until
D. unless

(xiv) I shut the door on Muggs ......
A. just on time
B. just in time
C. just at the time
D. just for the time

(xv) ...... a large marble clock, as well as several vases, on the mantelpiece.
A. It was
B. They were
C. There was
D. There were

(xvi) Muggs used to behave ...... he thought I wasn't one of the family.
A. as though
B. as when
C. as
D. so as

Rewrite the following sentences according to the instructions after each. Change the meaning as little as possible. Change only enough to do what you are asked to and to make a correct sentence.

(xvii) 'Muggs went up the backstairs and down the frontstairs and had me cornered in the living-room.'
Begin: 'Muggs cornered me ......'

(xviii) 'There was a slight advantage in being one of the family, for he didn't bite the family as often as he bit strangers.'
Begin: 'The slight advantage ......'

(xix) 'Mother had to throw a saucepan of cold water on him before he stopped.'
Begin: 'He did not stop ......'

(xx) In not more than 80 words, say what you think would be the disadvantages of owning Muggs, basing your answer on the author's account of his behaviour.

20 *On trial for murder*

As he rose to resume his cross-examination after lunch Sir Evelyn studied the witness's face attentively. The lad was very pale, even paler than he had been that morning, and possibly nearer to a real breakdown than at the time of his earlier rather theatrical display. But he must not underestimate this witness whose strength of will might be as deceptive as his strength of arm; he had made some headway with him and had extracted some damaging admissions, but not enough. He must strike more firmly: after the promise, the performance.

'We had reached the point this morning,' he began, 'when you had struck the blows and your father had rolled from off you to the floor?'

'Yes,' the witness said.

'And you thought that he was dead?'

'I was certain of it.'

'How certain? Did you look?'

'Yes, sir. And I listened. I couldn't hear his breath.'

'You looked and listened. Did you touch him?'

Rupert gave a small shudder of aversion and shook his head.

'You didn't feel his heart or anything like that?'

'Oh no.'

'You just assumed it. Your father was lying there; he might be living; he might be dead. And you didn't satisfy yourself for sure?'

'I didn't, I'm afraid.'

'I take it you were sorry for what had happened?'

'Sorry! I was horrified. I never meant to kill him.'

'You mean you hadn't done a crime?'

'Of course I hadn't.'

'And you *knew* you hadn't.'

'Yes, I knew. What I'd done I'd done in self-defence.'

'You *knew*,' Sir Evelyn repeated, brushing away the rest of the answer with a wave of his bony hand. 'And you've told us that you were sorry. Could I put it to you that you pitied him?'

'Naturally I did,' Rupert replied, with an expressive glance towards the jury.

'He was lying there, bleeding, was he not?'

'Yes, yes, he was.'

'Did you attempt to stem the blood?'

'No. What was the use?'

'Did you hold his head or try to make him comfortable?'

'No, I told you. I couldn't touch him.'

'Did you call for help?'

'No, no.'

'He wasn't dead, you see,' said the prosecutor gently.

'Perhaps not. He seemed so to me.'

'Why didn't you call for help?'

'Why! Because I panicked. Haven't I been telling you!' And the witness looked round the Court as though seeking allies against unreason.

'What were you afraid of?' continued the level, gentle voice. 'You'd committed no crime. You've told us so.'

'And I hadn't. I hadn't.'

'And you pitied this man. You've told us so.'

'I did.'

'Then, if that were so, why didn't you give the simple Christian help a man would give a dog that lay like that? Why didn't you tend him yourself or call for help?'

'I'd panicked. Oh, I've told you.'

'Why did you panic?' asked Sir Evelyn, raising his head slowly and fixing the witness with a long accusing stare. 'Was it because you knew you'd murdered him?'

from *Reputation for a Song* by GEOFFREY GRIERSON

In questions (i) to (xv) only one choice is correct.

(i) Sir Evelyn studied the witness's face
A. because he had turned pale
B. to see whether there was any chance of his breaking down
C. as he got up
D. hoping he would be attentive

(ii) Sir Evelyn was of the opinion that the boy
A. might be difficult to break down
B. might deceive him
C. might be very strong in the arm
D. might do some damage

(iii) Before lunch the witness
A. had hit his father
B. had rolled about on the floor
C. had described a fight he had had with his father
D. had described how his father had hit him

(iv) Rupert shook his head to indicate that
A. he hadn't heard his father breathing
B. he hadn't touched him
C. he hadn't looked at him
D. he hadn't felt his heart

(v) Rupert was sorry
A. for being afraid
B. for having apparently killed his father
C. for committing a terrible crime
D. for not feeling his heart

(vi) When the prosecutor pointed out that the boy's father had not been dead, the boy
A. agreed that he hadn't been
B. denied that he had been
C. said he believed that he had been
D. said he knew that he had been

(vii) The prosecutor wanted the witness to explain
A. why he had treated his father like a dog
B. why he had not helped him as even a dog would have
C. why he had been like a dog
D. why he had failed to give him the help most men would have given to a dog

viii) The reason the witness gives for not calling for help was that
A. he had acted without thinking
B. he knew he had murdered him
C. it was too late to help
D. he had been in a hurry

(ix) 'rather' (l. 4) means
A. somewhat
B. quite

C. very
D. fairly

(x) 'damaging admissions' (ll. 7–8) means that
A. the boy had said 'yes' many times
B. the boy had made statements that could go against him
C. the boy had made some dramatic entries into the courtroom
D. the boy had admitted doing a lot of damage

(xi) 'aversion' (l. 19) means
A. dislike
B. the act of turning away
C. fear
D. doubt

(xii) 'I'm afraid' (l. 25) means that the boy
A. was frightened
B. was sorry
C. was sorry for his father
D. regretted being afraid

(xiii) 'stem' (l. 40) means
A. check
B. remove
C. collect
D. hide

(xiv) 'so' (l. 47) means
A. to such an extent
B. therefore
C. dead
D. definitely

(xv) When Rupert replied (ll. 36–37) with an expressive glance towards the jury, he
A. gave them a look full of meaning
B. made an unhappy movement
C. caught a glimpse of them showing their feelings
D. tried to attract their attention

To answer the following, write down the number of the question and the letter of every item which could fill the gap. The items you choose must be grammatically correct and correspond to the meaning in the original passage.

(xvi) Sir Evelyn asked the witness ...... that his father was dead.
A. how was he certain
B. how certain was he

C. how certain he was
D. he was how certain

(xvii) Rupert said that he had killed his father ......
A. on purpose
B. unintentionally
C. intentionally
D. incidentally
E. carelessly
F. without meaning to

(xviii) Sir Evelyn asked Rupert ...... his father's head.
A. whether he had held
B. had he held
C. if he had held
D. whether had he held
E. he had held

(xix) Sir Evelyn ...... that Rupert knew he had murdered his father.
A. accused
B. asked
C. suggested
D. questioned
E. demanded

(xx) Describe in not more than 80 words what, in the prosecutor's view, the witness ought to have done and ought not to have done after he had struck his father.

21 *A frightening experience*

Ann turned into a wing of the house which was quite deserted and silent. At the end of it a shut door confronted her. She opened it softly. It was all dark within. But enough light entered from the corridor to show her the high bookcases ranged against the walls, the position of the furniture, and some dark, heavy curtains at the end. She was the first, then, to come to the meeting. She closed the door behind her and moved slowly and cautiously forwards with her hands outstretched, until she felt the curtains yield. She passed in between them into the recess of a great bow-window, opening on to the park; and a sound, a strange, creaking sound, brought her heart into her mouth.

Someone was already in the room, then. Somebody had been quietly watching as she came in from the lighted corridor. The sound grew louder. Ann peered between the curtains, holding them apart with shaking hands, and through that chink from behind her a vague twilight flowed into the room. In the far corner, near to the door, high up on a tall bookcase, something was clinging – something was climbing down. Whoever it was, had been hiding behind the ornamental top of the heavy mahogany bookcase; was now using the shelves like the rungs of a ladder.

Ann was seized with a panic. A sob broke from her throat. She ran for the door. But she was too late. A black figure dropped from the bookcase to the ground and, as Ann reached out her hands to the door, a scarf was whipped about her mouth, stifling her cry. She was jerked back into the room, but her fingers had touched the light switch by the door, and as she stumbled and fell, the room was lighted up. Her assailant fell upon her, driving the breath out of her lungs, and knotted the scarf tightly at the back of her head. Ann tried to lift herself, and recognised with a gasp of amazement that the assailant who pinned her down by the weight of her body and the thrust of her knees was Francine Rollard. Her panic gave place to anger and a burning humiliation.

She fought with all the strength of her supple body. But the scarf about her mouth stifled and weakened her, and with growing dismay she understood that she was no match for the hardy peasant girl. She was the taller of the two, but her height did not avail her; she was like a child matched with a wild cat. Francine's hands were made of steel. She snatched Ann's arms behind her back and bound her wrists, as she lay face downwards, her bosom labouring, her heart racing so that she felt that it must burst. Then, as Ann gave up the contest, she turned and tied her by the ankles.

from *The House of the Arrow* by A. E. W. MASON

In questions (i) to (xiv) only one choice is correct.

(i) When Ann entered the room she was able to see that it was empty
A. although the door was closed
B. because of the light coming through a gap in the curtains
C. because of the light coming through the open door
D. by switching on the light

(ii) She moved slowly forward with her hands outstretched
A. because that was the easiest way to pass between the curtains
B. because it was dark and she couldn't see
C. because she wanted to close the window
D. because she wanted to feel the curtains, to see what they were made of

(iii) How did she first know that someone else was in the room?
A. She felt someone behind the curtains
B. She watched someone come in from the lighted corridor
C. She heard someone come in through the open window
D. She heard someone moving in the room

(iv) When she looked through the curtains, she saw
A. someone climbing down the bookcase
B. someone hiding on top of the bookcase
C. someone standing on a ladder
D. someone standing in the corner near the door

(v) Ann ran for the door
A. because she was late for an appointment
B. in order to lock it

C. to see who the figure was
D. to get away

(vi) As Ann fell
A. she cried out
B. a scarf was put round her mouth
C. she turned on the light
D. her attacker turned on the light

(vii) Ann gave a gasp of amazement because
A. her attacker was someone she knew
B. she was trying to lift herself and couldn't
C. the scarf knotted tightly at the back of her head was hurting her
D. her attacker was driving the breath out of her lungs

(viii) During the fight Francine was helped by
A. a peasant girl
B. a wild cat
C. wearing special steel gloves
D. the scarf round Ann's mouth

(ix) 'confronted' (l. 2) means
A. opened
B. faced
C. interested
D. frightened

(x) 'brought her heart into her mouth' (l. 11) means
A. made her feel hungry
B. made her think of love
C. made her feel very frightened
D. made her feel sick

(xi) 'stifling her cry' (ll. 25–26) means
A. making her scream
B. making her shed tears of pain
C. preventing her from screaming
D. preventing her from breathing

(xii) 'she was no match for the hardy peasant girl' (ll. 36–37) means
A. she refused to light the latter's cigarette
B. the latter was the better fighter
C. the latter put out her cigarette
D. she was the better fighter

(xiii) 'her height did not avail her' (ll. 37–38) means
A. the fact that she was taller did not help her

B. the fact that she was taller did not prevent her fighting well
C. the fact that the other girl was on the ground helped her to win the fight
D. the fact that she was on the ground did not prevent her fighting well

(xiv) 'gave up the contest' (l. 42) means
A. won the fight
B. continued to fight
C. stopped fighting
D. fought harder than ever

To answer the following, write down the number of the question and the letter of every item that could fill the gap. The items you choose must be grammatically correct and must correspond to the meaning in the original passage.

(xv) ...... the door behind her she moved slowly forwards
A. Shut
B. By closing
C. While closing
D. Closing
E. Shutting

(xvi) She heard a sound ...... brought her heart into her mouth
A. who
B. which
C. what
D. that
E. it

(xvii) Ann was ...... Francine
A. taller as
B. as tall as
C. less tall than
D. taller than
E. greater than

(xviii) Ann felt that her heart ......
A. was going to burst
B. will burst
C. had burst
D. was about to burst
E. would have burst

Rewrite the following sentences according to the instructions after each. Change the meaning as little as possible. Change only enough to do what you are asked to and to make a correct sentence.

(xix) 'She turned into a wing of the house which was quite deserted and silent.'
Begin: 'The wing ......'

(xx) 'Ann tried to lift herself, and recognised with a gasp of amazement that the assailant who pinned her down by the weight of her body and the thrust of her knees was Francine Rollard.'
Do not use the first 'and'

(xxi) 'But the scarf about her mouth stifled and weakened her.'
Begin: 'But she ......'

(xxii) 'She snatched Ann's arms behind her back and bound her wrists, as she lay face downwards, her bosom labouring.'
Begin: 'Ann's arms ......'

(xxiii) Imagine that you were Francine. Give an account in not more than 80 words of what you saw and did.

22 *The witness*

She crossed the field and was just about to climb over the wall into the road, when she noticed a man in a car, drawn up stationary by the roadside and headed towards Gatehouse. The engine was running, and at that very moment, the driver pulled the car out across the road as though he was about to turn. At the same time, she heard another car approaching fast from the direction of Gatehouse.

The approaching car came very quickly round the upper bend, just as the first car turned across the road, blocking the way. There was a sharp squeal of brakes, and the second car stopped, slewing violently to the right and avoiding a crash by a miracle. The driver had shouted out something and the first man had replied, and then the driver of the second car had said in a loud and angry tone, 'Campbell! Of course! It would be Campbell' – or words to that effect.

Then there had been a sharp exchange of abuse, and Campbell had stopped his engine and got out. There was some sort of struggle and then, all in a moment, both men were out on the road, fighting and struggling. There were blows and a great deal of foul language. She could not see exactly what was going on, because the men were on the far side of the two cars. They had fallen to the ground and seemed to be rolling over one another.

When the struggle had gone on for some little time, she got a bad fright. A big spanner was flung suddenly into the air. It just missed her head and fell close beside her. She cowered down again under the wall, afraid to stay where she was and yet anxious to find out what was happening. After a little time she peered up again and saw something which frightened her still more. A man was getting up from the roadside, and over his shoulders he had got the body of another man. From the limp way in which it hung she thought the man must be dead. She didn't scream, because she was afraid if she did that the terrible man would hear her and kill her too. He carried the body over to the two-seater car and put it into the passenger's seat. This was the car which stood nearest to Gatehouse. She didn't see the face of the living man, because it was all bent down under the burden he was carrying, but as he passed in front of the lights of the four-seater to get to the other car she caught a glimpse of the dead man's face and it looked very dreadful and white. She couldn't describe it, except that she thought it was clean-shaven and the eyes were shut. The terrible man then got into the driver's seat and backed the two-seater away round the bend in the direction of Gatehouse.

from *The Five Red Herrings* by DOROTHY SAYERS

In questions (i) to (xii) only one choice is correct.

(i) After crossing the fields the girl
A. climbed over the wall into the road
B. headed towards Gatehouse
C. got into a car
D. saw a man in a car

(ii) The driver of the second car only avoided an accident by
A. shouting
B. stopping sharply
C. approaching quickly
D. blocking the way

(iii) The girl could not see the fight properly because
A it was very dark
B. the men were fighting inside one of the cars
C. the men were partly hidden by the cars
D. the wall was too high for her to see over

(iv) After the fight had gone on for some time
A. the men saw the girl
B. the girl was nearly hit by a flying spanner
C. one of the men fell close beside the girl
D. the girl fell off the wall

(v) When the girl looked up again she saw
A. one of the men lifting the other from the road
B. one of the men lying dead in the road
C. one of the men killing the other one
D. the dead body of one of the men hanging out of his car

(vi) The girl thought the man must be dead because
A. she had seen the other man hang him
B. she had seen the other man hit him with a spanner
C. the other man was carrying him on his shoulders
D. of how his body looked

(vii) The face of the terrible man was
A. clean-shaven and the eyes were shut
B. very dreadful and white
C. lit up by the lights of the four-seater
D. hidden from the girl

(viii) The terrible man drove away
A. because he was frightened by the girl's scream
B. after putting the body into the car
C. in the four-seater car
D. looking very frightened

(ix) 'blocking the way' (l. 9) means
A. going backwards
B. coming suddenly forwards
C. driving on the wrong side of the road
D. making it impossible for other cars to get past

(x) 'There were blows' (l. 19) means
A. the two men blew at one another
B. the two men struck one another
C. the wind was blowing
D. the men blew their noses

(xi) 'peered' (l. 28) means
A. looked
B. jumped
C. got
D. rose quickly

(xii) 'caught a glimpse of' (l. 39) means
A. touched
B. looked for a long time at
C. saw very clearly
D. saw for a moment

To answer the following, write down the number of the question and the letter of every item that could fill the gap. The items you choose must be grammatically correct and must correspond to the meaning in the original passage.

(xiii) The girl crossed the fields and ...... over the wall.
A. was just climbing
B. would just climb
C. was just going to climb
D. had just climbed
E. was on the point of climbing

(xiv) The driver pulled the car out across the road ...... he was about to turn.
A. as if
B. because
C. although
D. as
E. while
F. even if

(xv) The two men had shouted ......
A. at one another
B. from one to the other
C. to one another
D. at each other
E. one at another

(xvi) The girl was afraid that if the man had heard her scream, he ...... her.
A. had killed
B. should have killed
C. would have killed
D. may have killed
E. should kill
F. ought to have killed

Rewrite the following sentence. Change the meaning as little as possible. Change only enough to do what you are asked to do and to make a correct sentence.

(xvii) 'From the limp way in which it hung she thought the man must be dead.'
Begin: 'The limp way ......'

(xviii) Imagine that you were Campbell. Give an account of what you did, from the beginning of the story up to the point where you and the other man fell to the ground.

23 *A narrow escape*

The men were only two trucks away now and on both sides of the line. I could hear them panting over their exertions as they climbed up the sides of the trucks and stripped back the tarpaulins. Then something struck the side of the truck on which we were lying. A moment later the sliding doors below us were rolled back. There was a pause. They were evidently flashing a torch round the interior. One of the men muttered 'Nothing.' Then a boot grated on the bottom staple and a man began to climb up to the roof.

I listened to the man's feet as he clambered up. One, two, three, four . . . another step and the top of his head would be visible. We were caught. I waited for his shout. I wondered desperately whether it would not be better to stand up there and then and surrender. The policeman might not shoot. As I swallowed down the saliva that kept filling my mouth I saw that Zaleshoff had moved so that he was near the edge of the roof at the point where the man would appear. The next moment the top of the man's head came into view. He took another step and the white shape of his face appeared. At that moment Zaleshoff's left arm shot out and he grasped the man's collar. I saw his right hand jab the revolver against the side of the man's head.

It was done in the fraction of a second. With his hands grasping the staples on the side of the van he could not attempt to defend himself. I heard him give a stifled sob of terror. Then, too softly for me to hear, Zaleshoff whispered something to him. The next moment the man was climbing slowly on to the roof. I could see his face more clearly now. His mouth was half open and his eyes were moving quickly from side to side seeking some way of escape. He bent forward to steady himself by putting his hands on the roof. Zaleshoff lifted his right arm. I saw him twirl the revolver round by the trigger guard and grasp the barrel. Then he brought the butt down with all his strength on the back of the man's head. The man gasped once and slumped forward half on the roof and half off it.

'Pull him up,' whispered Zaleshoff.

I grasped the man's outstretched arms, and pulled. I saw Zaleshoff trying to draw the feet sideways on to the roof. It was difficult to exert any force while we were lying on our faces, but somehow we managed it. There was a movement from below and the policeman called up to know if there was anything to be seen on the roofs of the other cattle trucks.

Zaleshoff squirmed across the roof to the far side.

'Nothing,' he called. He slurred the word so that it was little more than a grunt.

There was a curse from below. I heard the doors of the next truck being rolled back. The unconscious man's head had begun to bleed profusely, and the blood was trickling slowly down the curved roof and soaking the shoulder of my overcoat. I tried to move, but Zaleshoff stopped me with a warning gesture. I heard the search go on to the third and then the fourth van. Then I saw Zaleshoff beckon. I edged across to him. He brought his lips close to my ear.

'We'll go down one at a time now,' he whispered. 'You go first. When you get to the ground turn right, away from them, and walk, *walk,* mind you, slowly and quietly along by the trucks. Keep close in to them. They'll miss this poor sucker any minute now, and we've got to get clear. I'll catch you up.'

With infinite care and feeling as conspicuous as an aeroplane caught in searchlights, I swung my legs over the edge of the roof, rolled over on my face and felt with my toes for the staples. A moment or two later I reached the ground.

from *Cause for Alarm* by ERIC AMBLER

In questions (i) to (xv) only one choice is correct.

(i) The author thought they were caught because
A. he could see the top of the head of a man who was climbing up on to the roof
B. he could hear four men climbing up on to the roof
C. he could hear a man climbing up on to the roof
D. he heard a man shout that he had seen them

(ii) As the man's face appeared
A. Zaleshoff shot him
B. Zaleshoff hit him with his revolver

C. Zaleshoff took away his revolver
D. Zaleshoff seized him and pointed his revolver at him

(iii) The man could not defend himself because
A. he was too terrified to do so
B. he needed his hands to keep his balance
C. he had no time to do so
D. he couldn't breathe because Zaleshoff was holding his collar so tightly

(iv) The man put his hands on the roof because
A. Zaleshoff told him to do so
B. he was seeking some way of escape
C. Zaleshoff was holding him by the right arm
D. he didn't want to fall

(v) It was difficult for Zaleshoff and the author to get the man completely on to the roof because
A. they were lying on their stomachs
B. the man kept moving his arms and legs
C. the policeman was watching them
D. the truck on which they were lying started to move

(vi) The author tried to move because
A. he heard the doors of the next truck being rolled back
B. his shoulder was uncomfortable on the curved roof
C. the man's blood was wetting his coat
D. the unconscious man was slipping slowly off the roof

(vii) Zaleshoff told the author they must get away from the truck because
A. they would soon be seen in the searchlights
B. the searchers would soon return to look for the unconscious man
C. the man might regain consciousness at any moment
D. he could see the searchers walking back towards the truck

(viii) 'panting over their exertions' (l. 2) means
A. breathing hard because of the efforts they were making
B. crawling over the roofs of the trucks
C. searching through the contents of each truck
D. breathing hard with excitement

(ix) 'surrender' (l. 13) means
A. jump down and run
B. creep quietly away
C. attack
D. allow ourselves to be captured

(x) 'twirl the revolver round' (ll. 29–30) means
A. fire the revolver at the man
B. aim the revolver at the man
C. turn the revolver round
D. transfer the revolver to the other hand

(xi) 'slumped' (l. 32) means
A. jumped
B. stepped
C. ran
D. fell

(xii) 'He slurred the word' (l. 42) means
A. he spoke indistinctly
B. he shouted
C. he spoke quietly
D. his voice trembled

(xiii) 'one at a time' (l. 52) means
A. together
B. at once
C. separately
D. in a moment's time

(xiv) 'with infinite care' (l. 57) means
A. rather carelessly
B. very carefully
C. very worried
D. it seemed to take a long time

(xv) 'conspicuous' (l. 57) means
A. invisible
B. quick
C. high above the ground
D. easily seen

To answer the following, write down the number of the question and the letter of every item that could fill the gap above it. The items you choose must be grammatically correct and must correspond to the meaning in the original passage.

(xvi) Then something struck the side of the truck ......
A. on that we were lying
B. that we were lying on
C. which we were lying on
D. where we were lying on
E. in where we were lying

(xvii) Another step and we ...... the top of his head.
A. would be able to see
B. should see
C. had seen
D. were able to see
E. were seeing

(xviii) The policeman ...... shoot.
A. was not allowed to
B. would perhaps not
C. may not
D. had not to
E. could possibly not

(xix) ...... the staples on the side of the van he could not attempt to defend himself.
A. As he was held on to
B. As he was holding on to
C. Since holding on to
D. For he held on to
E. Owing to holding on to

(xx) Imagine you were Zaleshoff. Write a connected narrative of not more than 80 words, and using your own words as far as possible, describing what you did while you were on the roof of the truck.

24 *Duel in Antarctica*

It was just after three when I sighted a small, black dot moving ahead of me on the pack ice. For some time the sledge tracks had been winding amongst black pools of half-frozen bits of ice towards a small iceberg caught in the pack, and it was against the sheer green slope of this iceberg that the figure of Bland showed like a small dot dancing in the white void. It was painful to try and keep my eyes on it, and dangerous because it tended to make me lose my balance. After I'd had one fall through not watching my skis and had got up again with great difficulty, I ceased to worry about the mark ahead and concentrated on ski-ing as fast as possible.

When I looked again the berg was much nearer, but there was no sign of Bland. Presumably he'd passed behind it. Or had he seen me? Was he lying in wait? I left his tracks and circled away to the north of the berg. I soon caught sight of him then, not half a mile away and moving along the flank of the berg, which was a long one. Between us the snow lay flat, like a sheet of white. I drove my sticks into it, thrusting forward on a line that would converge with Bland.

He had almost reached the end of the berg when he saw me. He stopped and then his voice reached me on the cold wind. He was shouting to me and waving his sticks. Just as his companions had done, he thought I was part of a rescue party.

I unslung my rifle then, cocked it and slithered forward with the ski sticks looped over one wrist.

Something in the way I moved towards him must have warned him, for he suddenly stopped shouting and stood quite still, staring at me as I advanced on him. I was getting close now, and though the snow-glare made it difficult for me to see, he was outlined against the final shoulder of the berg and a good target. But I was taking no chances. I closed on him steadily, just as I would have done an enemy ship.

'Who are you?' His hail came to me quite clearly and I realised I was getting into the shelter of the berg.

'Craig,' I yelled back, and there was an exultant feeling inside me and I saw him stare at me for a moment and then dive for the sledge and his gun. But he didn't get up again and a moment later the thin crack of a shot sounded across the snow. He was firing from the shelter of the sledge. I turned then and circled to the west of him, cutting off his line of advance and reaching the shelter of the western end of the berg. He fired at me several times before I was out of sight, but I was a moving target and his bullets vanished into space.

from *The White South* by HAMMOND INNES

In questions (i) to (xvii) only one choice is correct.

(i) When the writer saw Bland the latter was
A. dancing
B. leaning against an iceberg
C. moving over the ice
D. climbing the slope of an iceberg

(ii) The writer lost his balance because
A. he had spots swimming in front of his eyes
B. his eyes were hurting
C. he was worried about the danger
D. he was looking at Bland, and not where he was going

(iii) When the author looked again
A. he couldn't see Bland's tracks any longer
B. Bland had disappeared
C. Bland was waiting for him
D. Bland was much nearer

(iv) Bland
A. would have got near the end of the iceberg if he had seen the writer
B. saw the writer when he stopped
C. called to the writer as he stopped
D. saw the writer before he got right to the end of the iceberg

(v) Bland shouted to the writer
A. because he thought the writer had come to save him
B. because his companions were shouting
C. to draw attention to the fact that the writer had put his ski-sticks in the snow
D. to tell the writer he was near the end of the iceberg

(vi) Bland stopped shouting because
A. he had started staring at the writer
B. he became suspicious of the writer
C. the writer ought to have warned him
D. he saw something in the writer's way

(vii) The writer did not shoot at Bland as he advanced towards him because
A. he did not have any luck
B. he did not get the opportunity to do so
C. he wanted to make sure of hitting him
D. he had to warn Bland first, as Bland was standing still

(viii) Bland did not get up again because
A. he was looking for his gun
B. he wanted to protect himself from the writer
C. he had dived into the water
D. he had fallen into a crack in the snow

(ix) Bland failed to hit the writer because
A. he ran out of bullets
B. the writer was out of sight
C. he was affected emotionally too strongly to be able to fire straight
D. the writer was not standing still

(x) 'sheer' (l. 5) means
A. light
B. sparkling
C. well outlined
D. perpendicular

(xi) 'there was no sign of Bland' (ll. 11–12) means
A. Bland made no signal
B. Bland left no tracks
C. Bland was not to be seen
D. Bland stopped moving

(xii) 'presumably' (l. 12) means
A. certainly
B. possibly
C. no doubt
D. undoubtedly

(xiii) 'thrusting forward on a line that would converge with Bland' (ll. 17–18) means
A. following tracks in the snow that looked as if they had been made by Bland

B. hurrying in a direction that would lead the writer to Bland
C. running along guided by a rope that would lead to Bland
D. pointing the sticks in such a way that Bland would notice

(xiv) 'unslung' (l. 23) means
A. put away
B. took off my shoulder
C. fired
D. unloaded

(xv) 'closed on him steadily' (l. 30) means
A. moved nearer and nearer to him
B. firmly refused to answer him
C. aimed carefully at him
D. moved across the water towards him

(xvi) 'hail' (l. 32) means
A. drops of frozen rain
B. shape
C. face
D. shout

(xvii) 'cutting off his line of advance' (l. 39) means
A. advancing towards him
B. cutting the rope he was using to advance
C. getting in front of him to prevent him advancing
D. removing the rope towards which he was advancing

To answer the following, write down the number of the question and the letter of every item that could fill the gap. The items you choose must be grammatically correct and must correspond to the meaning in the original passage.

(xviii) After I ...... through not watching my skis, I ceased to worry about the mark ahead.
A. did have one fall
B. had felt once
C. had once felt
D. once felled
E. had fallen once

(xix) I had great difficulty ......
A. to get up again
B. again to get up
C. in order to get up again
D. for getting up again
E. in getting up again

(xx) ......, he thought I was part of a rescue party.
A. Like his companions
B. As his companions
C. In the way of his companions
D. In the same way as his companions
E. Similar to his companions

(xxi) He suddenly ...... and stood quite still.
A. stopped to shout
B. stopped and shouted
C. shouted, stopped,
D. ceased shouting
E. ceased and shouted

(xxii) Describe, in not more than 80 words, what Bland did from the time he saw the writer.

25 *The lion trap*

The lion was about four years old, young, and with all his fearful powers gathered at their peak. He had very little mane, what there was being of coarse, wiry, yellowish hair. He stood about forty inches at the shoulder, and from his nose to the dark tip of his twitching tail he measured about nine feet six inches. His pads, each about the size of a small plate, were firm, and the claws retracted in them were still thick with the blood of the zebra and of the man. He came out of the bush noiselessly, sniffing quietly and looking about him. Small beasts in the vicinity became still, cocked, as though springs within them had been wound up.

The lion walked through the thin grass, without fear, as if he owned the world, for there was nothing he feared here. There were men in this world and he had come to know something of them. They fell easily, he had discovered. He had killed two, one a woman walking near her village, but other men had driven him off. The other, he had eaten a part of and he walked on now in search of the man's body.

He found the smell of blood where his human victim had lain, and the heavy smell of many living men who had walked here. Once this smell had sickened and frightened him, but now it had a sweetness, like meat, which caused him pangs of desire to kill again. He searched the ground, but the man had gone. He could smell zebra meat and he glided softly towards it, into the thick bush. When he came to the gateway of the trap he stopped and, like a cat, he sniffed delicately, then growled low in his throat. There was something of man here, and though hungry, he was not hungry enough to lose his caution. He peered into the trap from where he stood and began to sniff with deep brutish snufflings, walking round the trap. When he returned to the gateway he stared in again, and after clawing the ground in a rage, coughing and spitting, he chewed furiously at a rock nearby, breaking off flakes of it and playing with them. He moved off again, as smoothly as flowing water, grunting until he reached another trap. Here again there was something of man. He visited each trap, and familiarity by now with that certain gateway, that dull gleam of the rifle barrel's metal, caused him to stand some way off and growl before the opening of the last of the traps he visited. He moved closer, breathing in the rank smell of the meat, and in a playful sensual fury he drew one heavy clawing pad down one of the upright poles of the gateway, tearing it like cloth. Then he flailed it with both sets of his foreclaws. He turned round, lashing his tail, struck the wire with its tip, and immediately there was a livid flash and an explosion and the bullet from the trap-gun thudded into the stones behind him. He uttered a low, coughing roar and sprang into the air through the darkness, landing in a bush, which he ripped to pieces in a paroxysm which paralysed every creature within hearing.

He went off at a swinging lope until he reached the escarpment, carrying on for another seven miles until he came to a cattle enclosure. He caught the thick hot breath of the huddled cattle, and, full of murder, he padded, round it, past the smoky hut of the herdsman, who sat dozing, his spear impaled in the ground between his legs.

from *The Year of the Lion* by GERALD HANLEY

In questions (i) to (xv) only one choice is correct.

(i) At the lion's approach all the small animals
A. left the area noiselessly
B. sprang into the bushes
C. remained motionless
D. gave alarm signals

(ii) The lion was in search of
A. a number of men who had attacked him
B. a zebra he had recently killed
C. the body of a man he'd half eaten
D. a woman who had walked unprotected near the village

(iii) Experience had taught the lion that
A. he could kill men without difficulty
B. that he owned the world
C. men were afraid of him
D. the smell of blood was frightening

(iv) When he reached the gateway of the trap he was cautious because
A. the body he had left there had gone
B. men had been there
C. he was not hungry
D. he unexpectedly smelled zebra

(v) The reason he stood some way off the last trap and growled was
A. that the trap looked like the others
B. it was the only trap with a rifle barrel
C. he was preparing to eat the meat
D. he was sickened by the smell of man

(vi) The gun fired
A. when his paw struck the upright poles
B. when his tail struck the wire
C. when he tore at the cloth
D. as he leapt into the air

(vii) When the lion approached the hut the herdsman
A. was asleep
B. was alert, waiting for the lion
C. was sitting, smoking
D. was gazing at his spear

(viii) 'gathered at their peak' (l. 2) means
A. high up
B. altogether
C. as effective as they would ever be
D. in a powerful manner

(ix) 'They fell easily' (l. 14) means
A. they had difficulty in standing
B. they could be overpowered easily
C. they were confident
D. they were easy to find

(x) 'he wasn't hungry enough to lose his caution' (ll. 26–27) means
A. he was not sufficiently suspicious
B. he wasn't hungry
C. he wasn't very careful
D. his hunger was less strong than his suspiciousness

(xi) 'familiarity' (l. 35) means
A. friendliness
B. lack of respect

C. previous knowledge
D. earlier use

(xii) 'once' (l. 20) means
A. on one occasion
B. previously
C. when
D. only one

(xiii) 'livid' (l. 43) means
A. of a bright bluish colour
B. very angry
C. active
D. clear

(xiv) 'within hearing' (l. 47) means
A. that was listening
B. that he could hear
C. that could hear well
D. near enough to hear

(xv) 'full of murder' (l. 51) means
A. carrying the body of a man he had killed
B. in pain
C. anxious to kill
D. still remembering the attempt to kill him

To answer the following, write down the number of the question and the letter of every item that could fill the gap. The items you choose must be grammatically correct and must correspond to the meaning in the original passage.

(xvi) The lion was about ......
A. four years
B. four years young
C. four
D. four years of age
E. aged four
F. the four years aged him a lot

(xvii) The lion had ...... that men fell easily.
A. found
B. invented
C. known
D. learnt
E. come to know
F. thought

(xviii) ...... a woman walking near her village other men had driven him off.

A. After killing
B. After to kill
C. After he had killed
D. Having killed
E. While killing

(xix) The smell of living men ...... kill again.

A. desired the lion to
B. made the lion want
C. wanted the lion to
D. made the lion want to
E. made the lion want that

(xx) Describe in not more than 80 words what the lion did from the moment he came to the gateway of the trap (l. 24) to when the gun went off (l. 44).

26 *A rough road*

Out on the road the jeep was already waiting. The governor's secretary had promised an experienced driver, but the boy hunched drowsily at the wheel looked scarcely above school age.

As I got in beside him, he sat up and started the engine. We set off with a jerk which scraped skid marks on the wet gravel. In a few minutes we were out of the town and heading at a tremendous pace in the direction of Bacalar. My hat blew away but when I asked him to stop, he refused. We were being followed by spies and it was necessary to drive fast to throw them off. I looked round. Although the road was straight for a couple of kilometres, no other car was in sight.

When we reached the junction I had noticed on the way out to the lagoon, we swung off to the left on to the new road, which was banked about twelve feet above the jungle. Its hard but uneven surface made the vehicle weave and bounce. To the danger of being catapulted off the embankment was added the discomfort of the cold, for at the speed we were travelling the keen air cut through my cotton shirt and trousers. I implored the boy to go slower, adding as an excuse that I wanted to look out for wild animals. He replied that the only animals we were likely to see were tapir. The faster we drove, the better our chance of coming up with them before they could run away. He had hardly spoken when the jeep struck a rain-filled pot-hole, which slammed a sheet of muddy water over the windscreen. Blinded, he braked sharply and the tyres ripped sideways into a skid. We stopped with one wheel over the embankment. When we got going again it was at a speed little faster than a walking pace.

As we drove deeper into the hills, the road surface became more treacherous. It was no longer banked up and in the hollows there were pools of flood water. His confidence now fully regained, the boy plunged the jeep through them, laughing at the wings of spray thrown up by the wheels. I asked him if the road became worse farther on. He replied that he did not know as he had never been so far along it before. He had been told that it was impassable, but I need not worry; he would get me through.

We had been driving about three hours and had covered seventy kilometres without seeing either people or dwellings. We had passed no vehicles, although in the softer patches the mud had been deeply rutted by trucks. With only ten kilometres to go, I was beginning to feel hopeful, when the track entered a broad depression.

At first we kept going with two wheels in a rut which was not quite deep enough to tip us over. Soon it became deeper. He stopped and changed into four-wheel drive. I urged him to back while there was still a chance of getting out, but he refused. We lunged on for a yard or two as he tried to swing the wheels out of the rut. He succeeded, but the jeep only slewed sideways and stuck with its nose bedded in a wall of mud. Now, too late, he put the gears into reverse. The tyres whined under us and we sank, toppling perilously. I kicked his foot off the accelerator and the engine stalled. In the silence the mud squeaked and gurgled.

from *One Man's Mexico* by JOHN LINCOLN

In questions (i) to (xv) only one choice is correct.

(i) While they were driving towards Bacalar the author
A. asked the boy to drive fast because they were being followed by spies
B. threw off his hat
C. refused to stop because they were being followed by spies
D. asked the boy to stop for his hat

(ii) The author implored the boy to go slower because
A. he wanted to look for wild animals
B. he was frightened that they might have an accident
C. his shirt and trousers had blown away
D. he had cut himself

(iii) They continued at little faster than a walking pace because
A. the boy had been blinded
B. the tyres had been ripped
C. one of the wheels had fallen over the embankment
D. they had only just avoided an accident

(iv) As they drove deeper into the hills the boy started to drive faster again because
A. there were pools of flood water in the hollows
B. he was laughing
C. he had regained his sight
D. he was feeling sure of himself again

(v) The author was told he need not worry, for
A. the road was impassable
B. the boy would get him through
C. the boy had never been so far along the road before
D. the boy did not know the road

(vi) After seventy kilometres the author was beginning to feel hopeful that
A. they might soon see another vehicle
B. they would manage to complete their journey safely
C. they had only ten kilometres to go
D. the track would enter a broad depression

(vii) They might not have got stuck if
A. the boy had put the jeep in reverse earlier
B. the jeep had stayed in the rut
C. the boy had not stopped and changed into four-wheel drive
D. the author had not kicked the boy's foot off the accelerator

(viii) 'drowsily' (l. 3) means
A. young looking
B. sleepily
C. with a mad look in his eyes
D. uncomfortably

(ix) 'to throw them off' (l. 10) means
A. to remove them
B. to throw them away
C. to put them off
D. to stop them following

(x) 'cut through' (ll. 18–19) means
A. penetrated
B. tore
C. cut off
D. ripped open

(xi) 'He had hardly spoken' (l. 23) means
A. he had shouted
B. he had spoken very softly
C. he had only just finished speaking
D. he had only said a few words

(xii) 'little' (l. 28) means
A. small
B. barely
C. almost
D. nearly

(xiii) 'treacherous' (l. 30) means
A. dangerous
B. wet
C. uneven
D. hilly

(xiv) 'urged' (l. 45) means
A. promised
B. tried to persuade
C. encouraged
D. forced

(xv) 'He succeeded' (l. 48) means he succeeded in
A. swinging the wheels out of the rut
B. lunging on for a yard or two
C. slewing the jeep sideways
D. bedding the nose of the jeep in a wall of mud

To answer the following, write down the number of the question and the letter of every item that could fill the gap. The items you choose must be grammatically correct and must correspond to the meaning in the original passage.

(xvi) As they drove along the embankment the author ...... the boy to go slower.
A. demanded
B. asked
C. suggested
D. persuaded
E. begged
F. hoped

(xvii) The road's hard but uneven surface ...... the vehicle to weave and bounce.
A. resulted
B. effected
C. made
D. caused
E. started
F. did

(xviii) ...... we drove into the hills the more treacherous the road surface became.

A. As further
B. The further
C. Further
D. The farther
E. As more
F. The for

(xix) When the author asked the boy if the road became worse farther on, he replied: ......

A. 'I did not know. I had never been so far along it before'
B. 'I don't know. I have never been so far along it before'
C. 'I don't know. I was never so far along it before'
D. 'I hadn't known. I had never been so far along it before'
E. 'I haven't known. I am never so far along it before'
F. 'He doesn't know. He has never been so far along it before'

(xx) In not more than 80 words, using your own words as far as possible, describe the unpleasant things which happened to the author during the drive.

27 *The early railways*

Those who welcomed the railway saw it as more than a rapid and comfortable means of transit. They actually saw it as a factor in world peace. They did not foresee that the railway would be just one more means for the rapid movement of aggressive armies. None of them foresaw that the more we are together – the more chances there are of war. Any boy or girl who is one of a large family knows that.

Whenever any new invention is put forward, those for it and those against it can always find medical men to approve or condemn. The anti-railway group produced doctors who said that tunnels would be most dangerous to public health: they would produce colds, catarrhs and consumptions. The deafening noise, the gloom, the glare of the engine fire, would have a bad effect on the nerves. Further, being moved through the air at a high speed would do grave injury to delicate lungs. In those with high blood-pressure, the movement of the train might produce apoplexy. The sudden plunging of a train into the darkness of a tunnel, and the equally sudden rush into full daylight, would cause great damage to eyesight. But the pro-railway group was of course able to produce equally eminent medical men to say just the opposite. They said that the speed and swing of the train would equalise the circulation, promote digestion, tranquillise the nerves, and ensure good sleep.

The actual rolling-stock was anything but comfortable. If it was a test of endurance to sit for four hours outside a coach in rain, or inside in fug, the railway offered little more in the way of comfort. Certainly the first-class carriages had cushioned seats; but the second-class had only narrow bare boards, while the third-class had nothing at all; no seats and no roof; they were just open trucks. So that third-class passengers gained nothing from the new mode except speed. In the matter of comfort, indeed they lost; they did, on the coaches, have a seat, but now they had to stand all the way, which gave opportunities to the comic press. This kind of thing: 'A man was seen yesterday buying a third-class ticket for the new London and Birmingham Railway. The state of his mind is being enquired into.'

A writer in the early days of railways wrote feelingly of both second- and third-class carriages. He made the suggestion that the directors of the railways must have sent all over the world to find the hardest possible wood. Of the open third-class trucks he said that they had the peculiar property of meeting the rain from whatever quarter it came. He described them as horizontal shower-baths, from whose searching power there was no escape.

from *Travel in England* by THOMAS BURKE

In questions (i) to (xvi) only one choice is correct.

(i) Those who welcomed the railway did so because
A. it was a convenient way of making a change
B. they expected more than just a quicker way of travelling
C. they realised it would not get faster or more comfortable for a very long time
D. they thought it would enable armies to be moved rapidly

(ii) All boys and girls in large families know that
A. the faster aggressive armies are moved the more chances there are of war
B. we are together more than we used to be
C. a lot of people being together makes fights likely
D. whenever there is a new invention there are always people to condemn it

(iii) The anti-railway group
A. tried to show that tunnels were certain to cause colds
B. said that tunnels would be cold
C. produced doctors who would show the colds they had caught in tunnels
D. would show people the colds and catarrhs they had got in tunnels

(iv) Those who wanted railways
A. claimed the railways would make people nervous
B. said people would sleep well if they travelled in trains
C. produced doctors who were all as good as each other
D. said sleeping well would become impossible without railways

(v) The railway
A. was not much more comfortable than a coach
B. attempted to a slight extent to prevent comfort
C. offered more comfort when people were testing how long they could sit outside a coach
D. was slightly less comfortable than a coach

(vi) Third-class passengers
A. found the trucks faster than the coaches but less comfortable
B. found the trucks as comfortable as the coaches, but found this had disadvantages
C. found that speed was the only fashionable thing about the trucks
D. found that after the introduction of railways the seats were taken away from coaches

(vii) The story that a third-class ticket buyer had the state of his mind enquired into was made up because
A. it gave a chance to humorous papers
B. he had been seen the day before
C. third-class trucks were so uncomfortable to travel in
D. the London and Birmingham Railway had not yet been built

(viii) A writer suggested that the directors of the railways
A. had travelled all over the world
B. ought to have known that hard wood was good
C. had tried to find very hard wood
D. should be sent all over the world

(ix) The open third-class trucks
A. had some strange goods on board that always got wet
B. always got rained into when it was raining
C. were fitted with shower baths
D. were always turned round in order to face the rain

(x) 'actually' (l. 2) means
A. at that time
B. even
C. at first
D. actively

(xi) 'the gloom' (l. 13) means
A. the darkness
B. the thundering
C. the bad air
D. the dirt from the engine

(xii) 'do grave injury' (l. 15) means
A. slightly harm
B. make it difficult to breathe
C. do serious harm
D. kill the person instantly

(xiii) In 'just the opposite' (ll. 20–21) 'just' means
A. only
B. almost
C. more or less
D. exactly

(xiv) 'anything but comfortable' (l. 24) means
A. not at all comfortable
B. varied a great deal but was comfortable
C. the only good thing about the rolling-stock was that it was comfortable
D. almost comfortable

(xv) 'fug' (l. 26) means
A. the cold
B. comfort
C. the dry
D. the hot and stuffy atmosphere

(xvi) 'searching power' (l. 43) means
A. ability to find trucks
B. stinging force
C. ability to find a way in everywhere
D. efficiency at revealing things

To answer the following, write down the number of the question and the letter of every item that could fill the gap. The items you choose must be grammatically correct and must correspond to the meaning in the original passage.

(xvii) They ...... a rapid and comfortable means of transit.
A. did not see it only as
B. saw it not alone like
C. were not alone in seeing it as
D. only did not see it as
E. saw it not merely as

(xviii) ...... new invention is put forward, there are medical men to approve or condemn.
A. Even when a
B. Always if any
C. Every time a

D. All times a
E. Each time a

(xix) Indeed they lost, ...
A. as it concerns comfort
B. as regards comfort
C. as comfort concerns
D. as far as comfort concerns
E. as far as comfort is concerned

(xx) In not more than 80 words describe the various advantages and disadvantages of the early railways as compared with coaches.